The Time-Life Gardener's Guide

ROSES

A
REDEFINITION
BOOK

TIME® **LIFE** BOOKS

Other Publications:

AMERICAN COUNTRY
VOYAGE THROUGH THE UNIVERSE
THE THIRD REICH
MYSTERIES OF THE UNKNOWN
TIME FRAME
FIX IT YOURSELF
FITNESS, HEALTH & NUTRITION
SUCCESSFUL PARENTING
HEALTHY HOME COOKING
UNDERSTANDING COMPUTERS
LIBRARY OF NATIONS
THE ENCHANTED WORLD
THE KODAK LIBRARY OF CREATIVE PHOTOGRAPHY
GREAT MEALS IN MINUTES
THE CIVIL WAR
PLANET EARTH
COLLECTOR'S LIBRARY OF THE CIVIL WAR
THE EPIC OF FLIGHT
THE GOOD COOK
WORLD WAR II
HOME REPAIR AND IMPROVEMENT
THE OLD WEST

For information on and a full description of any of
the Time-Life Books series listed above, please call 1-800-621-7026
or write:

   Reader Information
   Time-Life Customer Service
   P.O. Box C-32068
   Richmond, Virginia 23261-2068

This book is one of a series of guides to good gardening.

The Time-Life Gardener's Guide

ROSES

TIME-LIFE BOOKS, ALEXANDRIA, VIRGINIA

CONTENTS

Despite the testimony of poets, not all roses come with thorns. In fact, there are so many varieties of roses that just about any generalization about them has to be qualified in one way or another. What can be said without fear of contradiction is that roses have been cultivated as long as any garden plant—the Chinese were breeding them 5,000 years ago—and that no other flower generates as much excitement and affection as a well-proportioned, richly hued, deeply perfumed rose.

Each chapter in this volume provides detailed information on the raising and enjoyment of roses. In addition to down-to-earth instructions on preparing rose beds, watering and fertilizing, propagating and pruning, staking and winterizing, there's a lively introduction to the many branches of the rose family and a guide to readying exhibition-quality blooms for display at rose shows. You'll also find a zone map that tells you when it's safe to plant in your area, a comprehensive maintenance checklist, tips on how to combat pests and diseases, and a fact-filled dictionary of roses with more than 150 entries.

1
ALL MANNER OF ROSES

Symbol of love and beauty for thousands of years, the rose probably has more admirers than any other flower, and has been bred and crossbred into a dazzling variety of forms. There are climbing roses and bush roses, roses grown solely for the aristocracy of their blooms and roses that lead a double life as billowing hedges. There are roses that come with thorns and without, those that are scented and unscented, those that are as artlessly simple as the single aureole of petals that marks a wild rose and those complex roses that unfurl their buds over several days, presenting each day a new vision of loveliness, multipetaled, changing in color.

Despite their enormous variety, most roses are descended from a handful of classic types, some of them dating back to pre-Biblical times. And for all their varied forms, most require essentially the same kind of treatment. They need sun and a soil rich in nutrients that encourage healthy roots and blossoms. The plants should go into the ground early enough for the roots to become established before top growth starts—a planting time that varies with climate and geography. But planting time also depends on the form in which the rose is delivered. Dormant plants, delivered "bare-root," without soil, should go into the ground earlier than those that are potted in a growing medium when purchased. Full details on such matters are discussed on the following pages, along with the special handling required for growing roses in containers, and for using roses as a screen or a hedge.

Finally, although there is no mystery to growing roses, keep in mind that instructions will constantly refer to operations performed on rose *canes;* canes are the horticulturist's term for rose stems. Keep in mind too that many modern roses are actually two plants in one, a cultivated top grafted onto a sturdier root. The graft is visible as a thickening, knotlike growth at the top of the rootstock, and should never be tampered with. Depending on locale, this graft should be planted either slightly above or slightly below the level of the soil *(page 12)*.

CONDITIONING THE SOIL FOR A BETTER BED OF ROSES

Roses grow best in loose, loamy soil with good drainage and a slightly acid pH. For superior performance, amend and condition the bed before planting; then repeat the process every five years or so to give your roses a fresh lease on life.

The first step toward a better rose bed is to test a soil sample for pH level, nutrient content and texture. Send a sample to your state agricultural extension service or buy a soil-testing kit at a garden supply center and test the soil yourself.

The pH scale—which runs from 0 to 14—indicates the level of acidity or alkalinity of the soil. Neutral soil has a pH of 7. The lower the number, the more acidic the soil; the higher the number, the more alkaline the soil. A pH of 6.7 is ideal for roses. If testing indicates your soil is too acidic, you will need to add lime; to reduce excess alkalinity, add sulfur.

Roses require ample quantities of three major nutrients—nitrogen, phosphorus and potassium—for abundant flower production and overall health. Enriching a bed with organic fertilizers like rotted manure, compost, peat moss, blood meal and bone meal not only provides the required nutrients but also improves soil texture for proper aeration and drainage.

Clayey soil, which is too dense, will not drain fast enough; sandy soil, which is too porous, drains too quickly. Both extremes can be corrected by a generous addition of organic matter.

To save time, you can repair all soil deficiencies—in pH, nutrient content and texture—in a single operation. The ground should not be frozen or too wet. Use a rotary tiller or work in needed amendments by hand, using a time-honored method called double digging. This involves removing the top layer of soil, loosening the layer below (the root zone), amending both layers, and replacing all soil as shown at right and opposite.

The big white blossoms of 'French Lace', a floribunda, start blooming in midseason and repeat all summer. They draw sustenance from a bed of rich, loose soil that was turned just before planting, then covered with a layer of organic mulch.

DOUBLE DIGGING: FIRST OUT, LAST IN

Double digging consists of making a series of trenches and filling in each one with soil transferred from the next trench in the series. A layer of soil taken from the first trench *(below, right)* is set aside. The subsoil in that trench is broken up and amended; then a layer of soil from a second trench is transferred to the first trench and then amended. Digging, transferring and amending continue until the soil set aside from the first trench is used to fill the last trench *(large arrow)*.

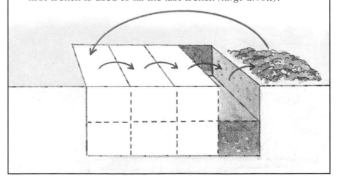

1 If you are starting a new bed, strip off any sod and discard it. Outline the bed with stakes and string or with chalk. At one end of the bed, use a spade to dig a trench; remove the top layer of soil to the depth of a blade length. Place the soil on a tarp. Mix the soil with organic matter, plus lime or sulfur if necessary, and set it aside.

2 With a garden fork *(left),* loosen the soil in the bottom of the open trench as deep as the length of the tines; this will make it easier for the plant roots to penetrate. Mix in organic matter, plus lime or sulfur if needed.

3 Dig a second trench parallel to the first and transfer the top layer of soil to the first trench. Amend the transferred soil. Loosen the bottom of the second trench and work in amendments. Repeat the process—opening a new trench, moving soil to the previously opened trench and amending—until you have conditioned the entire bed. Fill the last trench with soil removed from the first trench. □

CHOOSING BARE-ROOT ROSES AND PLANTING THEM RIGHT

Half the job of growing handsome roses is selecting trouble-free plants in the first place. This means checking them over carefully, starting with the roots. Most roses stocked by nurseries and mail-order houses, although grown in soil beds, are sold with bare roots—that is, with the roots removed from the earth and wrapped in peat moss and plastic. Undo the wrapping and look to see if there is any breakage. Minor damage that can be trimmed is acceptable; battered roots are not. The roots should also be firm, supple and moist; dry, brittle ones are clearly unhealthy.

Then examine the top part. The canes, or stalks, should also be strong and firm, and the buds must be dormant, looking plump but tightly closed. Roses showing signs of imminent blooms will not acclimate well and grow. Equally important are the so-called bud, or graft, unions. Many commercially available roses are cultivars, which means one sort of plant was grafted onto the rootstock of another. The sites of the grafting—where there are knots or swellings just above the roots—should be firm and solid. A soft, corky growth indicates a bacterial disease called crown gall, which is fatal to roses. If plants bought by mail order have badly damaged roots or indications of disease and rot, they should be returned for a refund. A problem plant seen in a nursery should not be bought.

A rose that passes inspection should have its roots soaked in water as soon as they come from the peat moss packing. They need a good drink before being planted, and at least 2 gallons of water per week for the rest of the growing season. (They need no watering in winter, when they are dormant.) The spot chosen for planting should be sunny; roses need an average of six hours of sun a day to prosper. And the ground itself needs to be well worked and rich. If the area has not been double-dug recently, the soil will require some attention. How to do this—and all the other steps in planting a rosebush—are shown opposite and on the following two pages.

A 'Trumpeter' rose—one of the floribunda hybrids —bursts with theatrically brilliant scarlet blooms. Planted bare-root in the early spring, floribundas quickly establish themselves in a garden and flower luxuriantly in about eight weeks.

1 Remove the packing around the roots. Soak the roots in a bucket of water for anywhere from two to 24 hours. While the roots drink, prepare the planting hole. If the earth where you intend to plant the rose has not been cultivated in the last year, dig a hole 18 inches wide and 18 inches deep; the roots need plenty of turned, enriched soil in which to grow. In already conditioned soil, the hole need be only 12 inches wide and deep. Set the soil aside.

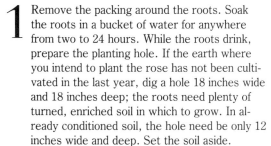

2 If the earth you have set aside is heavy and clayey, work in a trowelful of gypsum to improve the texture *(left)*. Sandy soil is all right; roses thrive in it. To enrich soil that needs further amending, combine a tablespoon each of blood meal and bone meal with 1 gallon of compost or humus and add them to the soil. Return about half of the mixture to the hole.

3 Make a cone-shaped mound of the soil you have returned to the hole. This will serve as a support for the plant, keeping it at the right height vis-à-vis ground level, and making it easy to spread out the roots in a circular pattern.

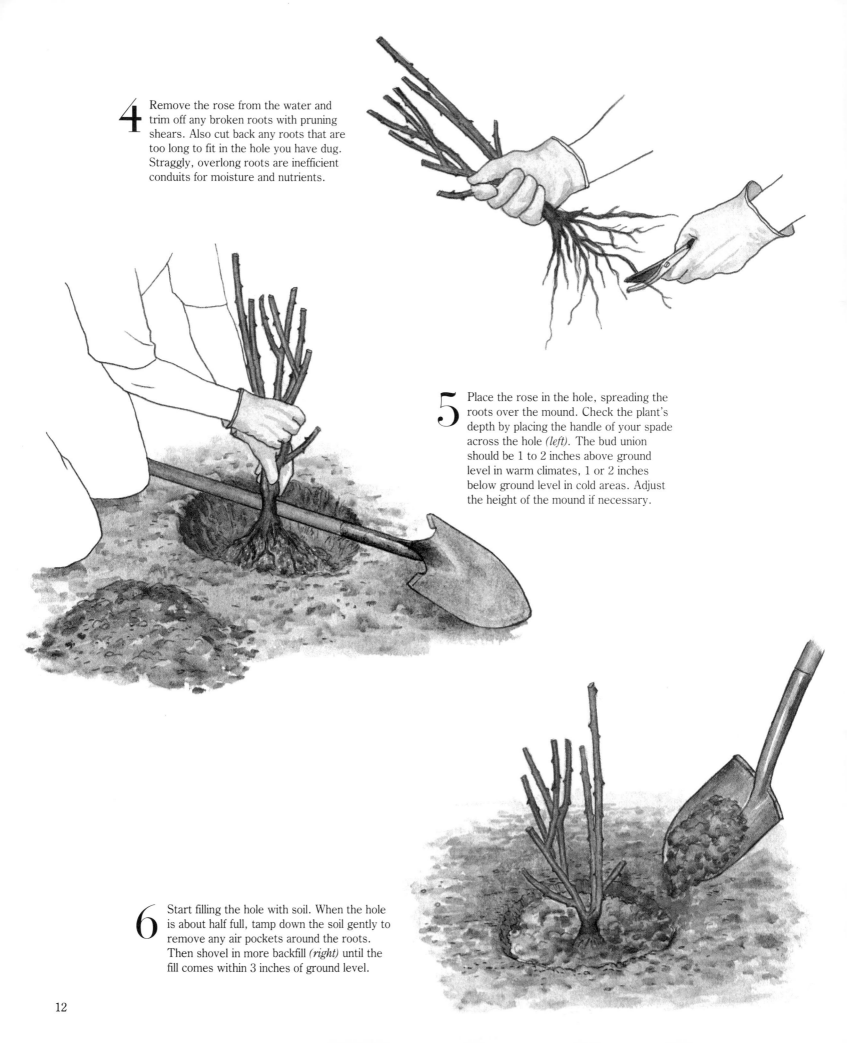

4 Remove the rose from the water and trim off any broken roots with pruning shears. Also cut back any roots that are too long to fit in the hole you have dug. Straggly, overlong roots are inefficient conduits for moisture and nutrients.

5 Place the rose in the hole, spreading the roots over the mound. Check the plant's depth by placing the handle of your spade across the hole *(left)*. The bud union should be 1 to 2 inches above ground level in warm climates, 1 or 2 inches below ground level in cold areas. Adjust the height of the mound if necessary.

6 Start filling the hole with soil. When the hole is about half full, tamp down the soil gently to remove any air pockets around the roots. Then shovel in more backfill *(right)* until the fill comes within 3 inches of ground level.

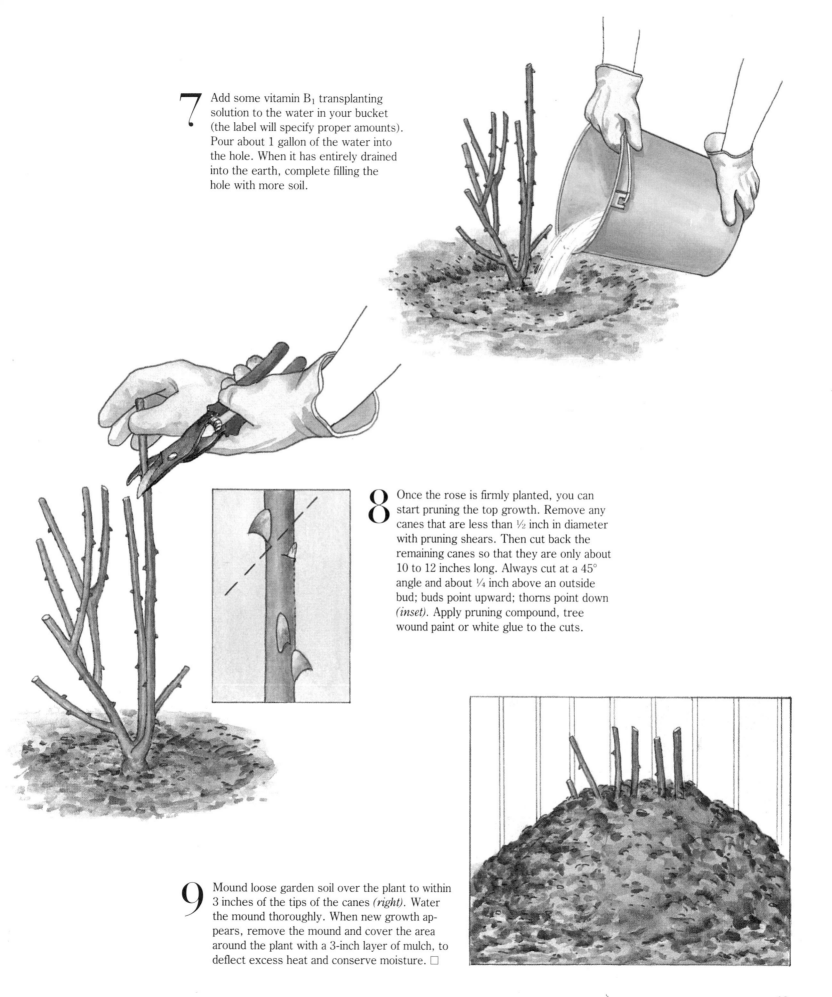

7 Add some vitamin B$_1$ transplanting solution to the water in your bucket (the label will specify proper amounts). Pour about 1 gallon of the water into the hole. When it has entirely drained into the earth, complete filling the hole with more soil.

8 Once the rose is firmly planted, you can start pruning the top growth. Remove any canes that are less than ½ inch in diameter with pruning shears. Then cut back the remaining canes so that they are only about 10 to 12 inches long. Always cut at a 45° angle and about ¼ inch above an outside bud; buds point upward; thorns point down *(inset)*. Apply pruning compound, tree wound paint or white glue to the cuts.

9 Mound loose garden soil over the plant to within 3 inches of the tips of the canes *(right)*. Water the mound thoroughly. When new growth appears, remove the mound and cover the area around the plant with a 3-inch layer of mulch, to deflect excess heat and conserve moisture. □

FILLING OUT A GARDEN WITH CONTAINER-GROWN ROSES

Container-grown roses are more expensive to buy than bare-root roses *(pages 10-13),* but they offer an advantage. Unlike bare-root stock, which must be purchased and planted early, container-grown roses may be planted any time during the growing season. That makes them useful as midseason additions or replacements.

Removal from the container is usually a simple matter of sliding out the root ball if the container is plastic *(opposite)* or peeling away the cover if it is paper. If the container is metal, it may be advisable to have the sides slit at the time of purchase to facilitate removal. If the container is made of biodegradable paper or fabric, it need not be removed; it will disintegrate in the soil.

Container-grown roses should be carefully inspected. First make sure the top growth is not diseased and that the canes show no signs of damage. If any leaves or buds have sprouted, they should be well formed and healthy. To make sure the plant is not pot-bound, inspect the holes at the bottom of the container; there should be no roots protruding from them. Then ask the nurseryman to pull the plant from its container so you can make sure the roots are not circling the root ball.

The key to the successful planting of a container-grown rose is its proper placement in the prepared hole. Since the nursery has already established the correct position of the bud union in relation to the soil surface in the container, it is important to maintain that relationship by planting the rose so that the top of the root ball is level with the surrounding surface after the hole is filled and lightly tamped.

A profusely blooming pale yellow 'Rise 'n' Shine' miniature rose borders a stone walk. Because of their diminutive size, miniature roses are easily grown and maintained in containers, and are often sold that way.

1 To plant a potted rose, use a trowel to dig a hole slightly wider and deeper than the pot *(right).* If the site was not prepared earlier, dig 6 inches deeper and fill the space with organic matter.

2 Carefully loosen the root ball by gently inserting the trowel around the edge of the pot *(above, left)*. Place one hand on top of the loosened root ball before turning the plant upside down to slide it from the pot in a single compact cylinder *(above, right)*.

3 Set the plant in the hole so that the root ball is level with the surface, removing or adding soil if necessary. Fill in around the root ball and tamp down with your hands *(below)*. Water thoroughly and add a layer of mulch around the base to retain moisture. □

A HEDGE OF SHRUB ROSES
FOR A BORDER

An informally shaped hedge of 'Simplicity' floribunda roses in bloom creates a bold pink and green border at the edge of a lawn—and provides privacy from the neighbors.

A hedge is a group of plants put to work in the garden. It can protect the garden boundaries, provide a backdrop for other plants or screen an unwanted view. It can also direct people to the path where the gardener wants them to go.

With their spreading shapes, shrub roses lend themselves well to use in informal hedges. Instead of being sheared as some formal evergreen hedges are, a rose hedge is allowed to grow naturally. After the hedge has been planted *(opposite)* a light pruning of straggling branches at the beginning of the growing season is all that is needed. Left on their own, shrub roses will then form a dense wall that will be spectacular when in bloom. Only occasional summer grooming may be necessary if the hedge is of a repeat-blooming variety *(pages 36-37)*.

Shrub roses are apt to come in bare-root form. For the best effect, use roses of one kind so that the shape and flower color are uniform the length of the hedge. In selecting a shrub rose, think not only about color, but also about the shrub's ultimate height at maturity and its growing habit—whether it will give you one big show of flowers or bloom repeatedly, whether it blooms singly or in clusters, whether it produces hips (or seedpods) that remain on the canes into the winter. For the characteristics of different roses, consult the Dictionary of Roses *(pages 100-151)*.

1 Before planting a hedge of shrub roses, mark off the area with stakes and string. Measure the length in feet and divide by 2 to calculate the number of plants you need; each rose plant needs 2 feet of room to spread.

2 While the bare-root plants soak in water (they should soak at least two hours before planting), determine where the planting holes should be dug. Use plant labels, stones or stakes as markers; place them 1 foot inside each end of the marked row and at 2-foot intervals between the two end markers. Plant as you would any bare-root roses *(pages 10-13)*. □

17

TRANSPLANTING TO GIVE A ROSE NEW LIFE

A rosebush that is otherwise healthy may fail to thrive because it stands in the shade of taller plants, or because its roots cannot compete for nutrients with the roots of nearby plants. By transplanting to a more hospitable environment, you can give a languishing rosebush a new lease on life. When a few precautions are taken, the procedure is so simple and safe that you may want to employ it for purely esthetic purposes—to brighten up a bare wall or fence, highlight a newly planted bed or revamp the design of your entire garden.

The key to success in transplanting roses is proper care of the root system, which should be kept moist at all times. The best time to transplant is in late winter or early spring, while the plant is dormant. With few if any leaves to keep supplied with water, the roots can devote most of their energy to the job of establishing themselves in the new site.

If you transplant early enough, the root system should be ready to support new foliage when warm weather triggers the next growth. Begin preparations as soon as the ground is workable. Water the plant thoroughly several days in advance; during the move the moistened soil will cling to the roots and help shield them from the drying effects of sun and wind. To further minimize the risks of exposure, wrap the root ball in a plastic sheet or a piece of burlap.

Follow the planting procedure for bare-root roses outlined on pages 10-13. Be sure to dig the new hole and prepare the soil before you lift the plant from the ground.

Transplanted from cramped quarters to a spacious location in spring, a young 'Keepsake', a hybrid tea rose, is established and blooming well before autumn leaves fall. Transplanting in late winter or early spring when they are dormant gives the plants time to adjust to a new site before they have to use their energy producing summer foliage and flowers.

1 After preparing the hole at the new site, loosen the premoistened soil around the rosebush. Use a shovel or a garden fork to dig a circle about 12 inches from the base of the plant and as deep as the shovel's blade or the fork's tines.

2 Gently lift the rose at an angle; support the root ball with the shovel or fork and guide it out of the ground with your free hand. Place a piece of plastic or burlap over the root ball and make it snug around the bottom *(left)*. Using the shovel for support, carry the rose plant to the prepared hole.

3 Lower the rose into the prepared hole. Pull the shovel and the plastic or burlap out from under the root ball, being careful not to disturb the roots. Backfill and water thoroughly. □

ROSES IN POTS
TO ENHANCE SMALL SPACES

Small and middle-sized roses—from miniatures and floribundas up to hybrid teas and grandifloras—can be planted in pots or other containers as well as in the ground. There are some big advantages to having roses in pots. For example, town-house dwellers with limited backyard space can have any number of potted roses on a deck or patio. Householders with bigger gardens can move clusters of pot-grown roses around for variety, or use them to provide color in areas where other plants have finished blooming. Gardeners in northerly regions can bring their potted miniature roses indoors for the winter —where they will thrive as houseplants until spring returns—and store larger plants in a garage or a cellar.

The pots need to be generous-sized so that the roots of the roses can grow. Containers 12 inches wide and deep are about right for miniatures and other small varieties; larger roses require 16-inch pots. Clay and plastic pots both work well. So do tubs made of decay-resistant woods such as cedar and redwood. Metal containers are out; they get too hot in summer. All must have drainage holes in the bottom to keep the roots from getting waterlogged. And once they contain roses, the pots need to stand on some sort of pedestal—a couple of bricks will do—so that excess water will not collect underneath.

Planting roses in containers, whether bare-root (pictured here) or container-grown, differs little from putting them in the ground (pages 10-15). The depth of planting varies slightly, however, and using a special potting mixture is vital. Making the proper soil mix and getting the depth right are shown below and opposite.

In a large terra-cotta pot on a brick terrace, the pink blossoms of a floribunda rise above a cascading purple lobelia. Growing in containers, the plants can be moved about from time to time to change the look of the garden.

1 To make the potting mixture that roses thrive on, combine 1 gallon of organic matter (peat moss, shredded bark and leaf mold) with ½ gallon of perlite, ½ gallon of vermiculite, 1 trowelful of superphosphate and ½ trowelful each of dolomite lime and trace minerals (manganese, zinc, sulfur, calcium, magnesium and iron) with 1 gallon of soil.

2 Transfer your potting mixture into the planting container until it is about three-fourths full. Then form a mound with the mix to accommodate the rose plant's roots. The top of the mound should be 2 inches or so below the container's rim. Trim off any dead or damaged roots, and spread the healthy roots over the mound.

3 Spread more mix over the roots until the mix reaches the bottom of the bud union—the knob where the stems or canes were grafted to the roots.

4 When you have finished planting, prune back the canes to about 6 inches long. Always make your cuts ¼ inch above an outside bud. Apply pruning compound to the cuts. Water the plant immediately, then give it a good weekly soaking. Roses should never dry out completely. It is also a good idea to apply some fertilizer, liquid or dry, every month or so. □

ROSES—
AN ANCIENT AND EXTENDED FAMILY

Shimmering with brilliant color, the petals of an 'Apothecary's Rose' look much as they did in medieval times, when this ancient plant was much prized by alchemists for its sweet and lasting perfume and for its medicinal properties; potions made from it were used to soothe upset stomachs and heal skin lesions. The 'Apothecary' is a member of the old strain of roses called gallica.

Part of the fascination of planting and nurturing roses is selecting which ones to put in the garden. The choices are rich and varied almost beyond counting. Mankind was cultivating roses at the dawn of history 5,000 years ago and has been busy at it ever since. The ancient Chinese bred roses, as did the Greeks and Romans; Europeans of the Renaissance made rose culture a quasi-religious passion. In more recent times, growers from many nations have steadily added more varieties by crossbreeding some of the earth's original wild roses, or crossing them with antique Oriental and European hybrids, or mating recent hybrids with older ones or with one another. The result has been untold thousands of varieties, many of them relatively new, others dating back to the Middle Ages and before.

The roses illustrated at right and on the following six pages show, first, the basic types of blooms and, second, the most interesting and significant classes—both historically and botanically—that are available today. From among them a rose enthusiast should be able to choose an intriguing mixture of the best, most beautiful and most fascinating of the world's roses.

THE FOUR TYPES OF BLOSSOMS

The blooms of all roses assume one or another of the four shapes or forms illustrated below. The main differences are in the number of petals—which varies from as few as five to more than 200—and in the petals' arrangement. It is from the arrangement—the number of petal layers—that the blossom types get their descriptive if not very elegant names: single, semidouble, double and very double.

SINGLE BLOSSOM

The simplest of rose blossoms, the single has five to 12 petals arranged on the same plane and not enclosing one another. All wild roses have single flowers.

THE SEMIDOUBLE

As its name implies, this sort of bloom is a halfway stop between a single and a double. It has two strata of 13 to 24 petals, but they are neither as numerous nor as closely furled as the petals in the true double.

DOUBLE FLOWER

A double flower has two complete and concentric rings of outer petals—and almost invariably a prominent central portion of more petals that encloses the pistils and stamens. The number of petals may vary from 25 or so to about 50 in the most lavish ones.

VERY DOUBLE BLOOM

Far the most extravagant-looking form of rose blossom, the very double grows anywhere from 50 to 200 small petals, which cluster in a number of tight rings or layers. It may be what rosarians call "button-eyed," having a single center formed by very tiny unopened petals *(above),* or be "quartered," having petals arranged somewhat like a pinwheel, in three, four or five separate clusters.

THE WILD ROSES

The earth's wild varieties, called species roses, are the ancestors of all the cultivated roses, and they continue to flourish around the world. In fact, 200 species of them still exist. Some grow as shrubs, some as climbers. All are hardy and they self-pollinate, producing seedlings that (unlike those of hybrids) duplicate the parent plant. The wild roses native to Europe and North America bloom only once a season, but those of the Orient bloom repeatedly.

SPECIES ROSE
Wild roses are always single, have only five petals and all show yellow stamens at the center. They can be showy, with bright shades of yellow, pink or red.

OLD GARDEN ROSES: THE HISTORIC CLASSES

The most ancient of the classes is one simply called China, which was bred by Chinese gardeners perhaps 5,000 years ago. The oldest of the European classes is gallica, which dates back at least to the first century A.D. It was only after traders brought Chinese roses back to Europe and crossbred them that Western roses became repeat bloomers. The finest and most important of the older cultivated roses are shown below, at right and opposite. Some have been favorite garden roses for many centuries.

GALLICA
Hardy plants that bloom once a season, members of the gallica family have single or double blossoms in pink, red, or red and white stripes. The Red Rose of Lancaster, symbol of one faction in the 15th-century Wars of the Roses, was a gallica.

DAMASK
An ancient class of roses brought from the Middle East to Europe by Crusaders, damasks are hardy and have double or semidouble blooms that may be white, pink or red.

MUSK

Named for their often strong musky fragrance, these roses have been cultivated in Europe and the Mediterranean basin for many centuries. Musks are hardy plants with arching canes and flowers that may be either single or double and either white or pink in color. Like most other old Western roses, they bloom only once in each growing season, usually in the spring.

CHINA

The most important variety brought to Europe from the Orient by British traders in the late 18th century, the China rose became popular both for crossbreeding and for its own small but decorative semidouble pink or red flowers.

TEA

Another ancient Chinese plant, the tea rose came to the West in the 19th century. It has been repeatedly crossbred with other varieties, producing today's large and varied class of hybrid tea roses. Not particularly hardy, the typical tea has large, showy blooms in lovely shades of cream, yellow and pink. Its fragrance suggests tea leaves, thus the name.

ALBA
Cultivated at least since the Middle Ages, alba is a natural hybrid of gallica and a Mediterranean species rose called *Rosa canina*. The alba produces a handsome show of blossoms that may be pale pink or white *(alba* means "white" in Latin) once a year. The White Rose that symbolized the House of York, enemy of the Lancastrians in England's Wars of the Roses, is thought to have been a cultivar known as 'Alba Semi-Plena'.

CENTIFOLIA
As the name implies, centifolias produce luxuriant very double blooms with 100 petals or more. They may be red, pink or white. These old roses, which date back to the 16th century, are also known as cabbage roses because their petals overlap rather like the leaves on a head of cabbage, and as Provence roses for a part of France where they were once widely grown.

MOSS
Originally a mutation of centifolia, this 17th-century rose is also hardy and produces similarly large, globular blossoms of pale pink or red. The difference is that the moss has patches of velvety green mosslike sheen on its sepals and stems.

PORTLAND

The first European rose to bloom more than once a season, it was originally bred in Italy by crossing damask and China strains, then brought to England, where it was named for an 18th-century rose fancier, the Duchess of Portland. The plant is not very hardy, but it produces lovely double blooms that may be pink, red or purple.

BOURBON

Another descendant of the damask and China classes, this rose was first grown by French colonists on the Isle of Bourbon in the Indian Ocean, then brought to France in the early 1800s. Bourbons are, like Portlands, repeat bloomers, producing single or double blossoms of white, pink, red or purple.

NOISETTE

First bred in 1828 by a South Carolina planter who crossed musk and China roses, the plant was soon taken to France by a man named Noisette, hence the rose's name. The flowers are quite varied, some cultivars producing single blooms, others producing very doubles, and the colors range from white through various pinks to purple.

HYBRID PERPETUAL

Among the most complex of older hybrids—their ancestry includes Chinas, Bourbons, Portlands and Noisettes—the perpetuals became the favorite garden roses of Victorian times for their ability to bloom more frequently than any roses bred in the West before. More than 1,000 varieties were bred then and perhaps 100 are still grown today. They are hardy plants, producing very double flowers of white, pink and maroon.

THE MODERN CULTIVARS

Over the last century and a quarter, botanists and rose breeders have developed the half-dozen new families or classes of roses shown here—the "moderns" that dominate today's plant catalogs and gardens. They are a varied group, ranging from splashy hybrid teas and large shrubs to small, adaptable miniatures. Most have been crossbred for hardiness as well as for beautiful blooms, and for increased resistance to disease. The modern cultivars come in a profusion of colors and forms, and most of them put on luxuriant, season-long shows of flowers.

HYBRID TEA

Among the best of modern roses, with their full, handsome blossoms, hybrid teas were also the first, dating back to 1867, when a French botanist crossed hybrid perpetuals with older tea roses. Hundreds of varieties of hybrid teas have appeared since. They are distinguished by their long stems and their flowers ranging in shape from singles to high-centered doubles and very doubles, and in color from white, pink and red to an unusual brilliant yellow.

POLYANTHA

Descended from China roses and an Asian species rose called *Rosa multiflora,* polyanthas are very hardy and produce large clusters of small flowers that may be single or double, and white, pink, yellow and even orange in color.

FLORIBUNDA

These roses, descended from polyanthas and hybrid teas, were first developed in Holland in 1911. True to their name, which means "flowering in abundance," they grow clusters of blooms—some of them rich very doubles—throughout the season. The blooms may be high-centered or cupped; the stems are long; the colors are white, yellow, orange, pink, red and lavender.

SHRUB

Answering a need for tall, tough, bushlike roses, the shrub varieties were first bred shortly after World War I from a wide mixture of antecedents. Some shrubs reach 10 feet tall, most at least 6, and all are very hardy, which makes them useful for many landscaping purposes. The blossoms are single to double and may be white, pink, red, yellow, orange or purple.

MINIATURES

The opposite of large shrub roses, miniatures reach only 10 to 18 inches in height and their blooms are to scale: clusters of small single to very double flowers varying from white to orange to purple. The first ones were bred early in this century by a Colonel Roulet from a dwarf Chinese rose that was later given the Latin name *Rosa rouletti* in his honor. They only became widely available, however, in the 1960s.

GRANDIFLORA

The newest class of roses, introduced in Great Britain in 1954, grandifloras are descended from hybrid teas and floribundas. The best varieties grow up to 10 feet tall and produce large double flowers in white, pink, red, yellow or orange. The first cultivar was 'Queen Elizabeth', named for the recently crowned Elizabeth II. □

2
COURTING PERFECTION

Roses typically reward their owners with such an amazing display of bloom that no amount of work involved in their care seems wasted. Indeed, much of it scarcely seems work at all, since it consists mainly of delicate adjustments in the plant's life cycle, performed with almost surgical precision. The care begins in the early spring, while the plant is still dormant, and lasts until about a month before the first hard frost. As with all plants, it involves a regular program of feeding and watering, and a rigorous program of spraying, for roses are prone to attack by mildew and fungus, and by pests such as aphids and mites and the infamous Japanese beetle. For some roses, such as tree roses and climbers, the routine chores include staking and tying. And, as winter approaches, almost all roses need some kind of winter protection, ranging from a simple mulch to elaborate wrappings and even, in the case of tree roses, to temporary interment underground. Finally, there are the season-long jobs of deadheading and disbudding, and the related job of pruning. More than mere plant maintenance, deadheading, disbudding and pruning are designed to improve the plant's appearance and its production of flowers. For roses that bloom repeatedly, constant deadheading is essential, and the process of disbudding is the magical manipulation that produces the spectacular roses that win prizes at rose shows.

Details of all these facets of rose care are explained on the following pages, along with their applicability to particular kinds of roses—for not all roses are equally demanding, and what benefits one rose may actively harm another.

A ROUNDED DIET FOR HEALTHY ROSES

Roses have hearty appetites. To keep on producing beautiful blooms, sturdy stems and healthy foliage, they require three indispensable nutrients: nitrogen, phosphorus and potassium. Fertilizer labels carry three numbers that give the percentages of nitrogen, phosphorus and potassium (in that order) that the mix contains. Only a soil test will tell you exactly what formulation is best for your garden. But the fertilizer most commonly used for roses is labeled 15-15-15, which means that 45 percent of the mix (by weight) consists of equal parts of the three main nutrients. The other 55 percent is filler, with traces of elements such as sulfur, calcium, magnesium, manganese, iron and zinc.

You can feed roses with granular fertilizer, spikes or liquid fertilizer. The granular and spike forms may release their nutrients at once or little by little; the liquids nourish the soil right away. Whichever you use, be sure to read the label carefully to find out how much to apply. Inadequate nutrition stunts growth; too much can weaken plants and make them susceptible to disease.

Roses should be fed on a regular schedule. Apply granular fertilizer at the start of the growing season, at the end of each bloom cycle (roughly six weeks) and nine to 12 weeks before the first frost in your area. One caution: if you have just planted roses in spring, give them time to establish themselves before starting to fertilize; young roots are fragile and can be burned if they are fertilized before they have time to establish themselves. Wait about four weeks before embarking on the schedule described above.

Time-release fertilizer delivers nutrients to the soil slowly but steadily over a four-month period. Apply it twice, once at the beginning and once again at the end of the growing season, six to eight weeks before the first frost.

During the bloom cycle and for special occasions, a supplemental dose of liquid fertilizer will brighten color and increase bloom size; results will be visible within 10 days.

Bursting with color and vigor, a 'Showbiz' rose beautifully demonstrates the value of a thoughtful, timely program of nutrition.

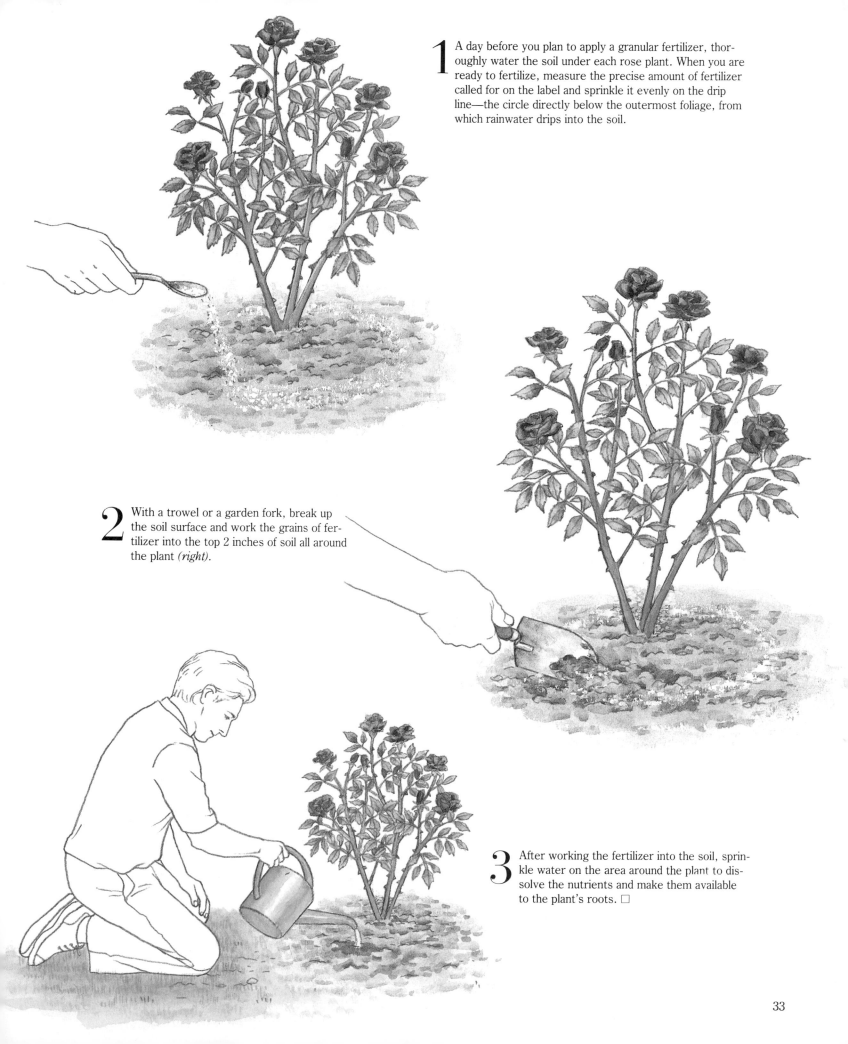

1 A day before you plan to apply a granular fertilizer, thoroughly water the soil under each rose plant. When you are ready to fertilize, measure the precise amount of fertilizer called for on the label and sprinkle it evenly on the drip line—the circle directly below the outermost foliage, from which rainwater drips into the soil.

2 With a trowel or a garden fork, break up the soil surface and work the grains of fertilizer into the top 2 inches of soil all around the plant *(right)*.

3 After working the fertilizer into the soil, sprinkle water on the area around the plant to dissolve the nutrients and make them available to the plant's roots. □

COMBATING DISEASES AND PESTS

There seems to be a law of existence that says the world's truly sublime things must all have at least one drawback—and roses are no exception. Some are peculiarly susceptible to pests and diseases. To help combat these afflictions, set up a steady program of maintenance. Always water roses by soaking the ground beneath them. Damp leaves are subject to diseases such as mildew and black spot. Keep the area around the plants well mulched to discourage weeds, which can harbor insect pests. Fertilize so that the roses are strong and able to survive diseases, and prune annually to open the plants' structure to the air. Remove any flowers, foliage or canes that show signs of infection and burn them. And clean any cutting tools thoroughly after use so that they do not spread infections.

Then come the chemicals. Roses should be sprayed twice during the dormant season, in late autumn and early spring, with a lime-sulfur solution that reduces fungus spores and kills insect eggs. During the growing season, spray every seven to 10 days with a fungicide, as a general protection against disease. At the first sign of insect or mite damage, apply a systemic pesticide; it will be absorbed in the plant tissues and thus kill many of the bugs that come along to feed on the plant. A strong spray of the hose from above can dislodge aphids and from below can dislodge mites. Ask a knowledgeable nurseryman about the safest sprays to use. Always read the instructions on the labels, including all the fine print, and follow them to the letter. When handling chemicals and spraying *(opposite),* always wear rubber gloves, goggles, a mask over your nose and mouth, and protective clothing—long pants, a long-sleeved shirt and solid work shoes. Do not spray on a windy day, just before rain or during a severe heat spell; wind and rain will carry the sprays away, and in temperatures above 80° F some sprays will burn plant tissue.

The delicate, silky petals of a floribunda rose called 'Cherish' unfold against a background of lush, glossy green leaves. Perfect blooms and foliage such as this, undamaged by insects or disease, show the benefits of judicious spraying with insecticides and fungicides.

1 To use a portable sprayer with a 1-gallon tank, pump-type handle, flexible hose and metal nozzle, first—in a separate container —dilute the recommended amount of liquid fungicide or insecticide with warm water (the ratio is often as little as 1 teaspoon of fungicide or insecticide to 1 cup of water). Then pour the mixture into the tank and fill the tank with water. Some insecticides and fungicides can be used in combination; check the labels. Do the mixing in the open air, to dissipate the chemical fumes.

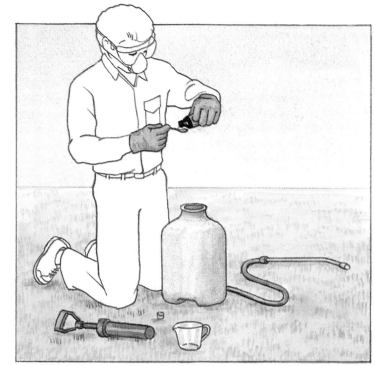

2 Tightly screw the lid with its plunger handle to the top of the tank. To pressurize the container, pump the plunger several times until it can no longer be pushed down.

3 Begin spraying by coating the top surfaces of the leaves. Work quickly; one good pass over each area should be enough. Then point the nozzle at the undersides of the leaves (right), where insects tend to congregate. Again cover the surface evenly. Use all of the solution you have mixed, and when you have finished spraying, clean the sprayer carefully and wash up immediately. □

TENDING ROSES
ALL SUMMER LONG

Every moment you spend in grooming your roses during the summer will be generously repaid with blossoms. Two methods of pruning—deadheading and disbudding—will encourage roses to flower longer and to produce larger or more abundant flowers.

Deadheading is the technique of removing faded flowers on repeat-blooming roses. Hybrid teas, floribundas and grandifloras all benefit from this technique. Remove the faded flower and a portion of the stem above the first strong dormant bud. This bud is located in the leaf axil of the uppermost set of leaves with five leaflets; leaves having fewer leaflets do not produce strong shoots. Once the dead flower is gone, the dormant bud will grow into a flowering shoot.

You should deadhead with every flush of bloom up until about three to five weeks before the first frost is expected. These last flowers should be allowed to produce rose hips, or seedpods, for the fall. Rose hips are not only attractive; they are also essential to the health of the plant. As the rose hips develop, the plant slows its growth and prepares for winter.

There are two exceptions to the standard procedure for deadheading. First, if you have a newly planted rose, remove just the flowers and leave the leafy stem during the first season of growth. Every available leaf is needed to manufacture sugar that will help build up the strength of the young plant. The second exception is with old garden roses that have only a single burst of bloom; the plants need to be allowed to develop their rose hips and therefore should not be pruned.

Disbudding is the act of removing certain buds to redirect the energy of the plant. To produce one large single bloom, pinch back all side buds and leave just the terminal bud. To produce a large flower cluster, do just the opposite: remove the terminal bud and leave all the side buds.

A 'Bahia' floribunda blossoms profusely in hues of salmon blended with rose. As long as the faded flowers are regularly removed, these roses bloom continually from midseason until the first autumn frost.

DEADHEADING

When a flower blossom is spent, use pruning shears and cut the stem at a 45° angle, ¼ inch above the first set of leaves having five leaflets. The dormant bud in the leaf axil *(inset)* will be stimulated to grow into a new shoot that will produce a flower within six weeks.

DISBUDDING

To encourage a terminal bud to grow into one large flower, pinch off any side buds growing below the terminal bud *(left)*. The earlier disbudding is done, the better. □

HYBRIDS AND CLIMBERS— BEDDING THEM DOWN FOR THE WINTER

Species roses, shrub roses and many old garden roses are hardy and live unharmed through the coldest Maine and Minnesota winters. But a majority of the modern hybrids such as teas, floribundas, grandifloras and large flowering climbers are highly sensitive to frigid weather. If hit with a deep North Country freeze, they can turn black and die virtually overnight. They need protection anywhere that winter temperatures get down around zero or below. To find out about temperature ranges and which roses require winterizing, consult the Zone Map *(pages 88-89)* and the Dictionary of Roses *(pages 100-151)*.

For the less hardy roses, winter preparations should begin right after autumn's initial hard frost. First comes some cutting back *(below)*. Then, in extremely cold areas, bush roses and especially tall tree varieties may need to be buried for the duration in a trench with a thick covering of earth *(pages 42-43)*. In regions with less punishing temperatures, rose plants can be adequately shielded simply by piling earth around the base. For more protection, a thick covering of leaves can be added. Both of these steps are shown on the opposite page. So is a method of using burlap to wrap climbing roses, which grow too tall for the earth-and-leaf method.

When spring comes, do not be hasty uncovering roses. An early thaw can bring out buds, which will be badly nipped if a last cold snap follows. Only when all danger of frost is past is it safe to uncover the roses. They should be pruned for spring and summer, as explained on pages 46-47.

Responding to the chill of autumn, a 'Bonica' shrub rose has produced hips, shed its leaves and dropped all but one blossom. Following the first hard frost, shrub roses can be cut back and protected for the onset of winter.

1 After the first frost, trim your rosebushes back until the canes are 1 or 2 feet in length. Do not worry about the location of buds (as you do in spring pruning); this fall cutting back, in reducing the size of the bush, lessens its vulnerability to drying winds and freezing.

2 Insulate the bottom portions of the canes, the bud union and the roots by mounding up 12 inches of loose, disease-free earth from another part of the garden. Firm the mound with your hands, but do not pack it down; crumbly soil aids drainage.

3 For still more insulation, form a cylinder out of a sheet of wire mesh and enclose your bush and its mound of earth in it. Fasten the mesh by bending the protruding horizontal wires around each other *(above)*. To make sure the cylinder stays put, pack another couple of inches of earth around the bottom of the wire.

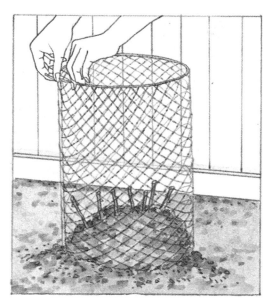

4 Pack the wire cylinder with mulch until it is almost full *(above)*. Old leaves, pine needles and bark chips all provide good insulation. In the spring, lift off the wire and the mulch and brush away the mounded earth. Then rinse off the canes with a light spray of water. □

A WINTER BLANKET FOR A CLIMBER

Climbing roses are too tall to bury underneath mounded earth or encase in wire cylinders. Still, their long canes need shielding from desiccating cold and wind. The best protection is burlap. First, pull the canes into a bundle at the base, leaving the tops pinned *(left)*. Wrap some twine around the lower 2 or 3 feet of the canes. Then wrap a burlap sheet around the tied canes, stretching it at least halfway up the plant. Tie the burlap in place with some more twine. In spring, remove the burlap, untie the canes and reposition the canes as necessary.

YEAR-ROUND CARE FOR TREE ROSES: SPRING STAKING, WINTER BURIAL

This pink-blossomed 'Duet', here grown as a tree rose and securely staked against the threat of high winds, commands a colorful mosaic of begonia beds and evergreen shrubs.

A tree rose is a standard made by grafting together parts from three different plants. The first provides the rootstock, the second a trunk and the third a flowering top. Perched on its slender "trunk," the top may reach a height of 3 feet, allowing you to bring the excitement of roses into a garden otherwise too small for ordinary rose plants.

You can buy tree roses at garden supply centers or by mail order. The flowering tops are usually cut from hybrid teas, floribundas or miniatures because they are compact and can be supported by long, thin trunks. Even so, the tops tend to be heavy, and tree roses are always at risk of bending or breaking in strong wind. They should therefore be supported with 1-by-1 stakes just after planting. Remove the stakes only when you are getting the plants ready for winter.

Although as a rule roses tolerate the cold better than most ornamentals, tree roses are sensitive to the drying effects of winter wind, sun and temperature fluctuations around the freezing point. And they cannot survive without protection where temperatures drop below 10° F.

The surest protection against wintry conditions is burial. After the first frost, cut back the canes to a length no greater than 2 feet, as shown on page 38. Dig a narrow ditch as long as the plant is tall. After loosening the soil around the roots, gently bend the trunk down until the entire plant is lying in the ditch. Backfill, then cover the plant with a mound of soil several inches high. If you expect subzero temperatures during the winter, cover the mound with several more inches of organic mulch or a plastic sheet. If you use plastic, weight it down with stones or pieces of wood.

In spring, when the ground has completely thawed and all danger of frost is past, remove the mulch and the soil, and gently raise the plant to an upright position. Firm the soil around the root ball. Stake as before; water and mulch. Prune as shown on page 47.

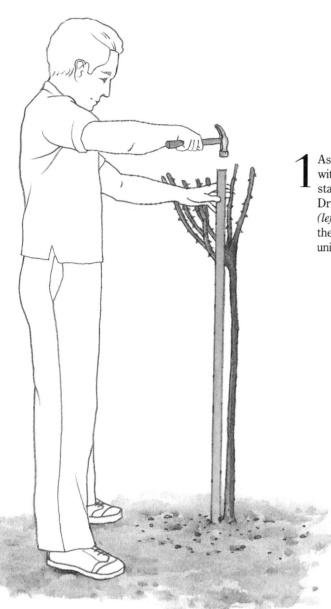

1 As soon as you plant a tree rose, support it with a 1-by-1 wooden or metal stake. Place the stake as close to the upright trunk as possible. Drive the stake about 1 foot into the ground *(left)*, so that the top of the stake is just below the upper bud graft (the swelling that marks the union between trunkstock and flowering top).

2 Secure the stake to the trunk by wrapping plant tape (the kind that stretches to let a plant grow) around the lower, middle and upper sections. Leave tape and stake in place at all times—unless you need to protect the plant for winter *(following two pages)*.

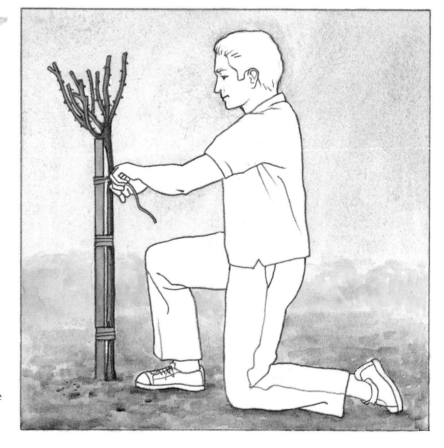

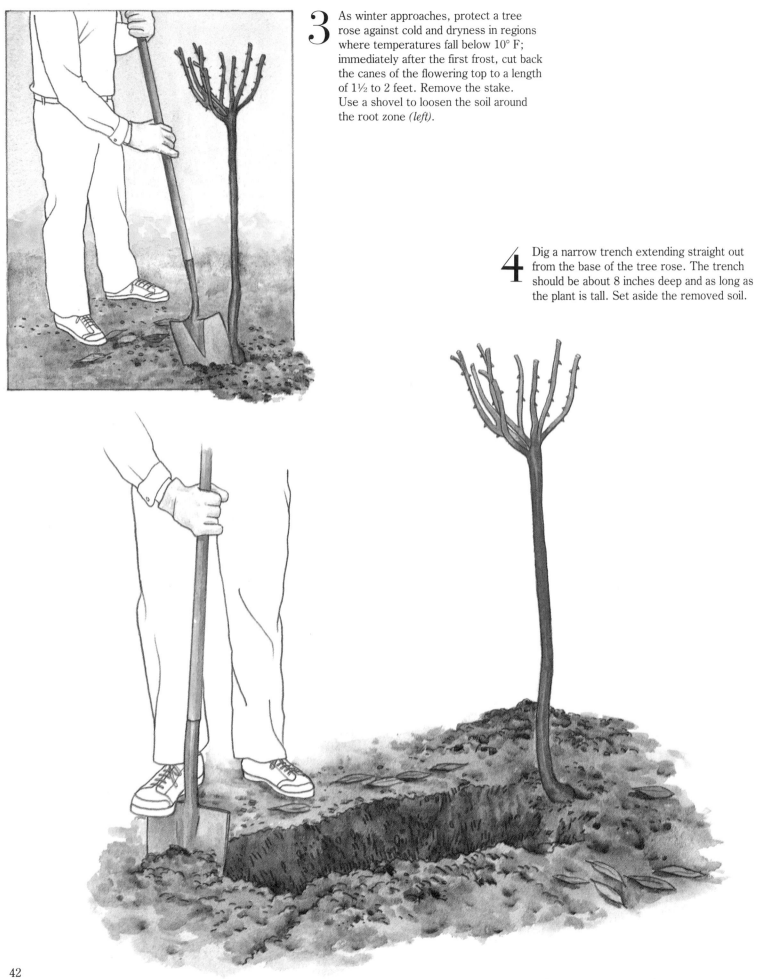

3 As winter approaches, protect a tree rose against cold and dryness in regions where temperatures fall below 10° F; immediately after the first frost, cut back the canes of the flowering top to a length of 1½ to 2 feet. Remove the stake. Use a shovel to loosen the soil around the root zone *(left)*.

4 Dig a narrow trench extending straight out from the base of the tree rose. The trench should be about 8 inches deep and as long as the plant is tall. Set aside the removed soil.

5 Grasp the middle of the trunk with your fingers and slowly bend the entire plant down into the trench *(right)*. Be careful not to break the trunk; if it does not bend easily, loosen some more soil around the roots.

6 Holding the trunk down with one hand, fill the trench with the soil you set aside and build a mound several inches high over the entire plant. Place extra soil over the upper bud graft, where the top of the tree rose joins the trunk. Firm down the mound with your hands. In very cold areas, add a layer of mulch or a plastic sheet weighted with sticks or stones. ☐

TIMELY PRUNING FOR HARDY ROSES

Although all roses can benefit from regular pruning, the extent and timing vary with different types of plants. Roses that flower on year-old growth, including shrub roses, species roses, and such old garden roses as gallicas, damasks, centifolias, Noisettes, Bourbons and Portlands, are usually hardier than their hybrid relatives and require less care. Pruning in the early spring, as the buds begin to swell, will make even the sturdiest specimen healthier and more attractive. As soon as you have finished pruning, resume the watering you suspended while the plant was dormant; new growth will wilt if it has insufficient water.

The first pruning target should be dead, diseased and damaged canes. Discolored and rough-textured, they are easily spotted among green, smooth-textured healthy canes and should be completely removed or cut back to good wood.

The next target should be unproductive canes, especially those that crowd each other or are too weak and spindly to produce flowers. Removing them opens the plant's interior to air and sunlight while permitting plant energy to be concentrated on productive growth.

Finally, judicious pruning can also improve the shape and the flowering potential of plants. A uniform trimming of all cane tips and a more severe pruning of lateral canes promotes outward growth and a greater quantity of blossoms.

When pruning roses, always wear leather gardening gloves for protection against thorns, and use sharp, clean tools.

Pruning shears can handle most cuts; loppers may be needed for large canes, and a thin pruning saw is best for use in tight and hard-to-reach spaces. Cuts that are ½ inch or more in diameter should be given a protective coating of pruning compound or white glue.

A handsome 'Golden Wings' shrub rose—upright, compact, with healthy new growth and a profusion of blooms—shows the effects of regular annual pruning in early spring.

1 To remove an entire cane, cut it from the base *(right, and designated A in the large drawing opposite)* at a 45° angle so that rainwater will run off. Use pruning shears for small canes, loppers for canes more than ½ inch in diameter.

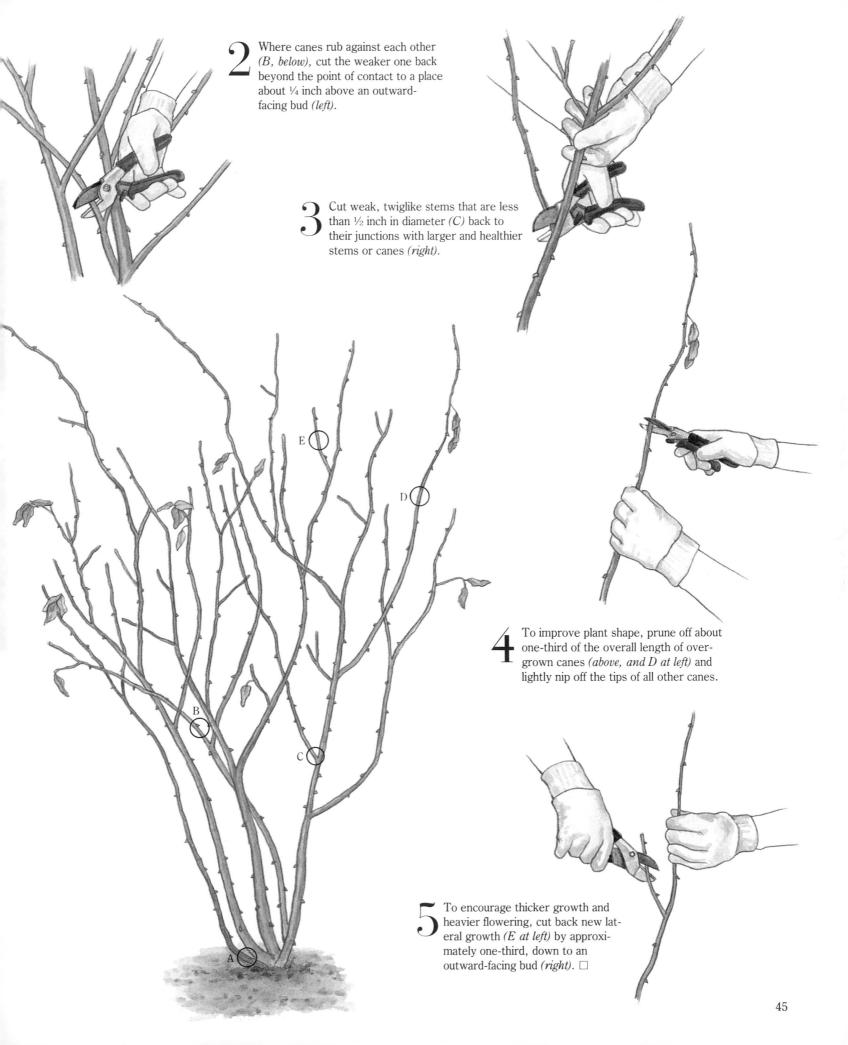

2 Where canes rub against each other *(B, below)*, cut the weaker one back beyond the point of contact to a place about ¼ inch above an outward-facing bud *(left)*.

3 Cut weak, twiglike stems that are less than ½ inch in diameter *(C)* back to their junctions with larger and healthier stems or canes *(right)*.

4 To improve plant shape, prune off about one-third of the overall length of over-grown canes *(above, and D at left)* and lightly nip off the tips of all other canes.

5 To encourage thicker growth and heavier flowering, cut back new lateral growth *(E at left)* by approximately one-third, down to an outward-facing bud *(right)*. □

PRUNING TO BRING OUT THE BEST IN MODERN ROSES

Since modern roses such as hybrid teas, polyanthas, floribundas, grandifloras and miniatures flower only on new wood, vigorous pruning is necessary to get the most out of each blooming season. The ideal time to prune such roses is in early spring, just before the growing season.

First, discard all dead, diseased or damaged canes, and any that are less than ½ inch in diameter should be removed; thinner than that they will neither support new growth nor produce any quality blooms. Then thin out the remaining canes to open up the plant and force it to concentrate its energy on a few young, strong canes. While thinning, keep in mind that you are also determining the shape of the plant for the summer.

Next, cut back the remaining canes to about two-thirds of their original length. To encourage new growth in the proper direction, place each cut ¼ inch above an outward-facing bud. Always cut at a 45° angle so that rainwater will run off instead of collecting on the wound. For larger, exhibition-quality blooms, you can shorten canes to one-third of their length—but be aware that such severe pruning may also shorten the plant's life span; in reducing the plant's foliage, you rob it of sugar it needs for strength and vigor.

Look closely at the pith, or center, of each cane. Any discoloration is a sign that the cane has been damaged by frost. Cut back a little more until the pith shows a solid cream color.

Once the growing season begins, you will have to keep a sharp eye out for suckers—robust shoots that emerge from the rootstock below the bud graft. Left unchecked, they will sap a plant's energy. The best way to remove suckers is to rip them off at the base.

The first result of early spring pruning, a 'Tiffany' hybrid tea rose blooms on new wood at the tip of a carefully cropped cane.

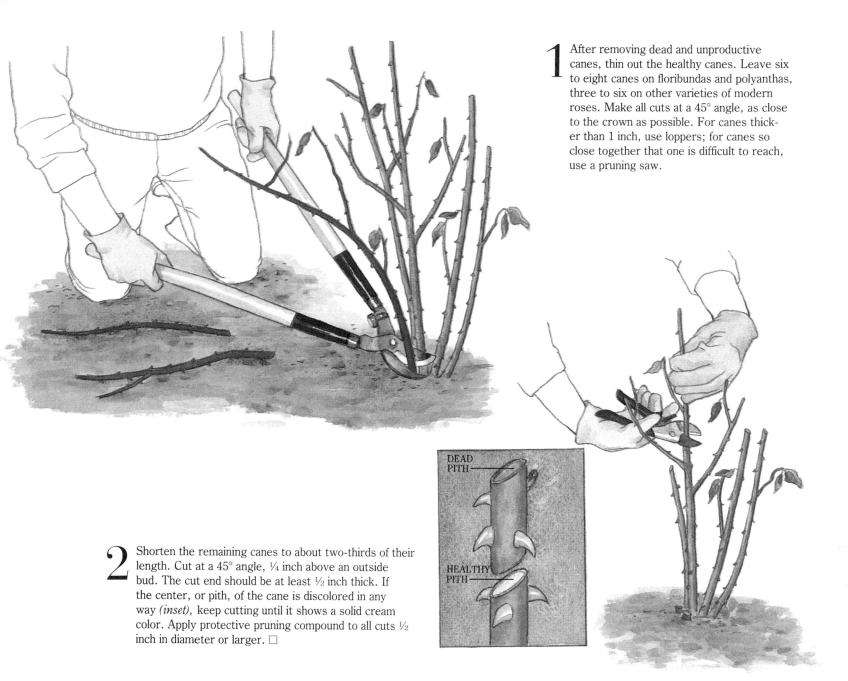

1 After removing dead and unproductive canes, thin out the healthy canes. Leave six to eight canes on floribundas and polyanthas, three to six on other varieties of modern roses. Make all cuts at a 45° angle, as close to the crown as possible. For canes thicker than 1 inch, use loppers; for canes so close together that one is difficult to reach, use a pruning saw.

2 Shorten the remaining canes to about two-thirds of their length. Cut at a 45° angle, ¼ inch above an outside bud. The cut end should be at least ½ inch thick. If the center, or pith, of the cane is discolored in any way *(inset),* keep cutting until it shows a solid cream color. Apply protective pruning compound to all cuts ½ inch in diameter or larger. □

DEAD PITH

HEALTHY PITH

THE WAR ON SUCKERS

Energy-draining suckers—stems that grow from a rootstock and do not share the desirable characteristics of the top growth—should be removed when they are a few inches long. Otherwise, they will eventually dominate the plant. Attempts to control suckers with shears or loppers are bound to end in frustration; they will only grow back. Instead, use a trowel to expose the base of the sucker where it attaches to the bud graft; then take hold of the sucker with both hands and rip it off the rootstock.

CLIMBING ROSES
FOR A WALL OF BRIGHT COLOR

Hardly anything that can be grown in a garden looks more dramatic than a rose plant laden with blooms growing up a wall, a weathered wooden fence or a trellis. Climbing roses provide bright, graceful spreads of color that can camouflage an unsightly view.

Persuading roses to climb in an eye-pleasing fashion, however, sometimes presents a problem. The term "climber" is misleading; with some exceptions, roses do not climb of their own accord. Unlike vines, they produce no tendrils that cling, and rose canes cannot twine about a trellis. In short, roses need help to climb well—some pruning, training and tying (opposite). The main requirement is that the plant have long, supple canes.

After the climber is well established in the ground—but before training begins—some pruning is called for. It should be done at the start of the growing season. Remove all unproductive canes (pages 44-45) and cut some of the laterals—the stems that branch off the main canes (or basal canes) back to the second bud; pruning encourages the remaining two buds to develop. When training time comes, there is an interesting fact to remember. The vertically growing canes of most climbing roses produce flowers only at their tips. But canes that are bent to grow horizontally produce blooms all along their length. It is not fully understood why this occurs, but the reason has to do with a botanical phenomenon known as apical dominance, which means that terminal buds—those formed at the branch tips, which naturally grow upright—dominate plant growth and inhibit lateral buds from developing. When the canes of a rose bush are spread out, the lateral buds face upward and are therefore able to bloom. Thus, when training a rose up a trellis or a fence, if you bend a number of canes toward the horizontal, you will get a richer, brighter panoply of flowers.

Its growth encouraged by having its canes trained horizontally along a wooden fence, a choice climbing cultivar called 'Joseph's Coat' produces extravagant clusters of blossoms. The rose was named for the Biblical garment of many colors because its flowers combine several tones of yellow, pink and red.

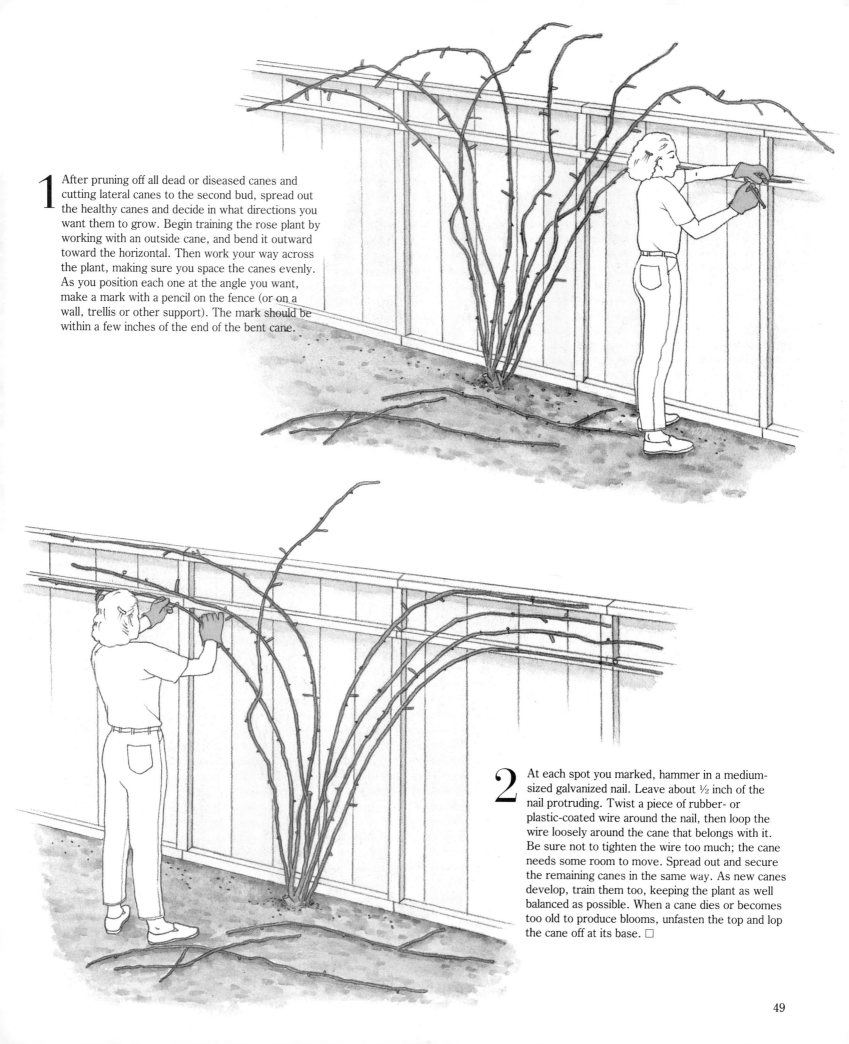

1 After pruning off all dead or diseased canes and cutting lateral canes to the second bud, spread out the healthy canes and decide in what directions you want them to grow. Begin training the rose plant by working with an outside cane, and bend it outward toward the horizontal. Then work your way across the plant, making sure you space the canes evenly. As you position each one at the angle you want, make a mark with a pencil on the fence (or on a wall, trellis or other support). The mark should be within a few inches of the end of the bent cane.

2 At each spot you marked, hammer in a medium-sized galvanized nail. Leave about ½ inch of the nail protruding. Twist a piece of rubber- or plastic-coated wire around the nail, then loop the wire loosely around the cane that belongs with it. Be sure not to tighten the wire too much; the cane needs some room to move. Spread out and secure the remaining canes in the same way. As new canes develop, train them too, keeping the plant as well balanced as possible. When a cane dies or becomes too old to produce blooms, unfasten the top and lop the cane off at its base. □

3
BEGETTING
MORE ROSES

Sooner or later, most gardeners who take roses seriously are tempted to try their hands at creating a new rose or duplicating an old favorite. They embark on a botanical adventure that may or may not yield the desired results, but that is likely to be fascinating every step of the way. Propagating roses is not child's play, but neither is it a secret rite. It uses familiar tools and materials, and simple procedures.

Roses can be started from seeds collected at the end of the growing season, when the seedpods, called rose hips, have ripened. The seeds will need to be put through a speeded-up version of their natural life cycle—softened in water and chilled in the refrigerator—before they can be planted. Simpler and quicker is the method of acquiring new plants from stem cuttings taken during the growing season. Treated with hormones to hasten the production of roots, the cuttings will be ready for transplanting, as tender seedlings, into individual pots in about six weeks. In a similar but more leisurely procedure, called layering, the growing canes are buried beneath the soil until the following year, when they will have sprouted roots, and can be lifted and cut from the parent plant. And ready-made new plants can also be acquired simply by lifting and moving the suckers that sprout around an existing rose plant—but plants grown from suckers will breed true only if they are taken from roses that have not been grafted.

The most fascinating way to produce a new rose, however, is by cross-pollination, the process of linking two different roses at the moment of conception. Cross-pollination is not difficult, but the timing is critical. The pistils of the host rose must be prepared for pollination at exactly the right stage of development, and must be dusted with pollen from the stamen of the mate before bees, hummingbirds or stray breezes take over the job.

For all of these methods of propagation, which are explained in detail on the following pages, only a few simple precautions are in order. Tools must be scrupulously clean; the growing medium must be sterile. And most of the methods presuppose the gardener's willingness to engage in a botanical gamble.

HYBRIDIZING—
A HOBBY FOR THE ENTHUSIAST

A homegrown hybrid, the handsome soft pink rose above combines the vigor of one parent, a cultivar named 'Pristine', with the long-lasting bloom of the other parent, 'Granada'. In general shape the flowers resemble those of both parent plants, but have higher centers than the blossoms of either.

Generations of botanists and rose growers have cross-bred thousands upon thousands of different cultivars (so called because they are varieties produced by careful cultivation). The best ones have been a boon to rose lovers: hardy and disease-resistant strains, tall climbers and decorative dwarfs, plants that produce exquisite double blooms and many more. Most of the blossoms exhibited today at rose shows are from hybrid cultivars, and hybrids dominate modern rose gardens.

But nothing says that breeding new cultivars has to be left to experts and professionals. Any amateur who has two different roses to cross-pollinate can make a hybrid. The techniques required are shown at right and on the following two pages. What is involved in essence is that rose blossoms are bisexual and include both the plant's main reproductive parts, the male pollen-producing stamens and the female pistils *(box, opposite)*. If the stamens are removed, the rose cannot reproduce itself. But if the pistils are brushed with male pollen from a different rose, the female plant will be able to reproduce—providing all goes well—and its offspring will be a hybrid combination of both parent plants.

One key to cross-pollinating is selecting blossoms that are just opening, to catch them before they pollinate themselves. Also, hybridizing should be done in the early spring so the female plant's seeds, should they germinate successfully, will have the entire growing season to ripen. Then comes the excitement of watching the seedpod swell, removing and planting the ripe seeds *(pages 56-57),* and finally seeing the resulting seedlings grow and produce flowers. The brand-new hybrid may be wholly unremarkable, or it may prove an outstanding combination of its parent cultivars like the lovely rose in the photograph at left. A successful plant can be propagated by grafting *(pages 60-63),* and possibly sold as a unique and valuable cultivar to a commercial rose grower.

ANATOMY
OF A ROSE BLOSSOM

The female parts of a rose, the delicate pistils, grow in the center of a blossom *(right)*. The stigma at the top of each pistil secretes a sticky substance to which the male pollen adheres. Sperm from the pollen travel down the stalk, or style, to the ovary, which bears the plant's ovules. The simpler male parts, the stamens, have stalks, or filaments, and, at their tips, pollen-filled sacs called anthers.

Beneath the stamens, pistils and petal-like sepals lies a rose's fruit, called a hip *(inset)*. This is where the seeds that will produce a new rose mature. If a bloom is pollinated successfully, the hip swells, then in about three months turns color (red, yellow, orange or brown) as the seeds inside ripen. If pollination fails, the hip does not swell but dries up and falls off.

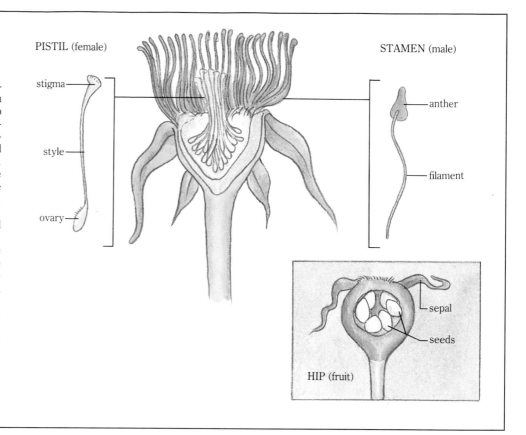

PISTIL (female)

stigma

style

ovary

STAMEN (male)

anther

filament

sepal

seeds

HIP (fruit)

1 To prepare a rose blossom that will play the female part in hybridizing, leave the bloom on its stem but remove all the petals with your fingers *(below)* by snapping them off. This exposes the stamens and pistils. If the tips of the pistils are sticky and yellow with pollen, discard the blossom; it is already pollinated.

2 After removing the petals, take small sharp scissors and gently snip off the stamens—the male, pollen-bearing stalks—that surround the female pistils *(box, previous page)*. You must remove all the stamens so that the doctored bloom retains only its female pistils. Through all these operations, the female bloom must be handled carefully so that it remains securely on its stem.

3 Cover what is left of the blossom with a small paper bag, fastening it so that the bag does not harm the pistils. The covering protects them from insects and any unwelcome breeze-blown pollen. After a day or two, remove the bag and examine the pistils to see if they have secreted their sticky, pollen-holding substance; if so, they will look moist. If they have not, replace the bag and let it remain on the rose for another day or two.

4 When the pistils have secreted their sticky substance, remove the bag. Cut from its stem the blossom that will provide the male pollen and snap off the inner petals so you can reach the stamens. Then, using a small, soft painter's brush, gather the yellow, powderlike pollen from the stamens *(above, left).* Turning to the female flower, brush the pollen *(above, right)* onto the female blossom's stigmas.

5 When you have finished the cross-pollination, again cover the female flower with a bag for protection. Next, write the names of the two cultivars you have used on a label with plastic-covered wire attached. List the female first, then the male, as in 'Peace' × 'Las Vegas'. Include the date. Secure the bag with the tag. After a few days, remove the bag. If the cross has taken, the hip will have started to swell. It will be ready to harvest in a few months. □

ADVENTURES WITH PROPAGATION: ROSES FROM SEEDS

Raising roses from seed is not for everyone—or for every rose. Although species roses such as *Rosa multiflora* breed true to type, a plant raised from the seed of a modern cultivar cannot be counted on to inherit the desirable characteristics of its mixed parentage. But if you like adventure, creating new cultivars from seeds you have collected and sown can be fun.

The seedpods, or rose hips, are ripe and ready for harvesting when they turn from green to another color—red, yellow, orange or brown, depending on the variety. But for best results, the seeds must be treated to break their dormancy before you sow them.

The treatment, known as stratifying, is simple enough. Soak the seeds in water overnight, then store them in a moist, cold place such as a refrigerator for six weeks. This process imitates nature; the combination of cold and moisture softens the seed coat, stimulates the embryo inside and hastens germination.

After being stratified, seeds should be sown immediately. Use flat containers or small pots and fill them with a moist, loose, sterile, soilless growing medium such as perlite, vermiculite, sand or peat moss. Containers may be made of clay or metal, so long as they have sufficient drainage holes.

To prevent damping-off, a fatal fungus that attacks young roots in wet soil, spray the growing medium with a diluted fungicide solution. Moisten the soil. Cover the container with a clear plastic bag and place it in a sunny location where the temperature remains around 70° F.

Separate and transplant the seedlings *(pages 58-59)* when the second pair of leaves (the true leaves) appears.

By late autumn the ripening hips of this species rose have turned from green to glossy red and begun to wrinkle, signs that they are ready for harvesting. The seeds inside can be treated to germinate and produce new plants.

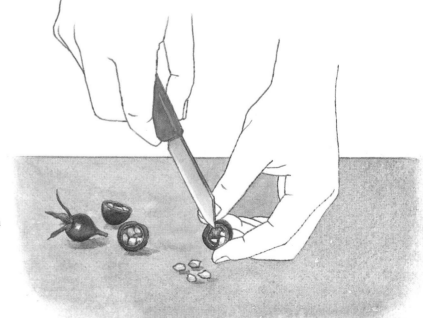

1 Pick a ripe rose hip, one that has lost all trace of green color. Cut it in half with a knife and pry out the seeds. Depending on the variety, some hips contain as many as 50 seeds; others hold only one or two. Select the plumpest seeds for stratifying.

2 Soak the seeds you have selected in a bowl of water overnight. The next day, discard any floating seeds; the more viable seeds will have sunk to the bottom *(left)*. Pour the water through a strainer, remove the seeds from the strainer and place them in a plastic bag that contains moistened peat moss. Label the bag with the seed variety and the date; seal it airtight and store it in the refrigerator.

3 After six weeks, remove the plastic bag from the refrigerator. Spread the peat moss on a clean surface and carefully pick out the seeds with your fingers *(below)*. Don't be surprised if you find that some of the seeds have already started to sprout.

4 Fill a container with a sterile growing medium to within 1 inch of the rim. Spray the surface of the medium with a diluted fungicide. Lay the seeds on the surface at intervals of 1 inch *(below)*, then cover them with ¼ inch more of the medium. Spray the surface with more diluted fungicide.

5 Water until the medium is completely moist, then cover the container with a plastic bag to create a minigreenhouse *(above)*. Place the covered container in a warm, sunny room; a temperature of 70° F is ideal. Check daily with your fingers to make sure the medium remains moist; add water as necessary. When true leaves appear—in about three weeks—the seedlings are ready to transplant. □

TRANSPLANTING SEEDLINGS INTO POTS

Situated on a patio, a young rose plant started from seed indoors begins its adjustment to life outdoors in an individual pot. After about 10 days of gradually increasing exposure to the elements, the rose will be ready for planting in the garden.

Rose plants started from seeds are surprisingly precocious growers. After only six weeks or sometimes less, the seedlings will have begun to crowd their original container and need transplanting. They will not yet, however, be rugged enough to go outdoors. The answer is an interim move from the container to small individual pots. A sure sign that the seedlings have rooted is the appearance of the first true leaves—the second pair each plant will produce. As growth progresses, the new leaves often look reddish before they turn green. They will be ready for transplanting when the leaves of one seedling start brushing against those of another.

The watchwords for transplanting are care and caution. As shown opposite, the delicate root systems should be handled as gently as possible, and the seedlings' stems should not be touched at all. The new individual containers ought to be at least 2½ inches across at the top. Terra-cotta and plastic pots both serve—as long as they have drainage holes in the bottom—and peat pots can also be used. They should be filled with the same moist, soilless growing medium used for starting the seeds *(pages 56-57)*.

After being transplanted, the seedlings will benefit from a dose of diluted fungicide, mixed and sprayed according to the instructions on the bottle, then from regular gentle waterings and occasional boosters of diluted fertilizer. The seedlings should stay in the pots until they are about 1 foot tall.

At that point, if they are going to be garden growers and not houseplants, they will need to be acclimated to outdoor living. Move them onto a porch or terrace for a couple of hours the first day, a couple more on the second and so on. After 10 days or so, they will have adjusted and can remain in the sun and wind. Then, to transplant them successfully from their pots into the ground, follow the instructions on planting container-grown roses on pages 14-15.

1 To lift up a seedling, use a small trowel or a spoon and dig carefully around and underneath the roots. Cradle the freed root ball with your other hand, keeping as much soil around the roots as possible. If you need to support the top of the seedling, take hold of the leaves, not the stem, which is easily bruised.

2 Place the seedling in a clean pot that contains soilless growing mixture. The top of the root system should be about ¾ inch below the top of the pot. Firm the mixture with your fingers *(right)* and add more if necessary. Water the seedling with a dilute solution of liquid fertilizer—just enough to moisten the potting mixture. Then spray the seedling with diluted fungicide to prevent the disease called damping-off, to which young seedlings are susceptible.

3 Place the seedling on a windowsill or other sunny, protected area. Ideally, the temperature should stay at about 70° F. Water when the planting mixture begins to look dry—the soil should be moist but not soggy —and supplement the water with diluted fertilizer every two weeks. The seedling will grow fast; it may reach 1 foot in height in as little as three weeks' time. □

BUD GRAFTING
TO DUPLICATE A FAVORITE HYBRID

Grafting roses sounds like a job best left to professional growers or botanists. But grafting is in fact surprisingly easy to do and, further, is the only workable way to propagate choice hybrid cultivars. Trying to grow hybrid roses from seed is an uncertain proposition because the seeds will not necessarily reproduce the desired qualities of the parent.

Grafting involves little more than taking a bud from the cultivar and attaching it to a rose of another, hardier species. The key to the process is finding this parent plant, or understock, as rose fanciers call it. The plant should be one that produces good strong roots. Favored as an understock, or rootstock, today is *Rosa multiflora,* whose roots are remarkably disease-resistant and will tolerate many types of soil. If you already have a multiflora or other usable understock growing in the garden, you can use it for grafting. Or one can be bought from a nursery—or even started from cuttings *(pages 64-67).*

The actual grafting is a relatively simple matter of doing a bit of cutting and fitting with a knife and some elastic tape. All the necessary steps are shown on these and the following two pages. This sort of grafting —called T budding from the shape of the cuts made in the understock—should always be done in early summer, when the cambium, a layer just under a rose's bark, is full of growth cells. Joining the cambium belonging to the bud to that of the understock is what makes a graft take hold and produce a fresh, new copy of the cultivar.

The only potential problem with T budding is a legal one. Hybrid roses are protected by 17-year patents that prevent anyone from propagating and selling them without permission from the person who first bred them. There is no reason, however, why a cultivar cannot be cloned for private use and enjoyment.

The grandiflora 'Gold Medal' displays the best of two worlds—lush gold blossoms and the sturdy rootstock of a hardier variety. Hybrids are best propagated by bud grafting because their seeds do not breed true.

1 To begin the grafting process, snip a healthy shoot from the rose you are planning to reproduce. The shoot should be young and fresh-looking but mature enough to have flowered. Wearing gloves to protect your hands, cut off about 12 inches of the shoot measured from the top leaves.

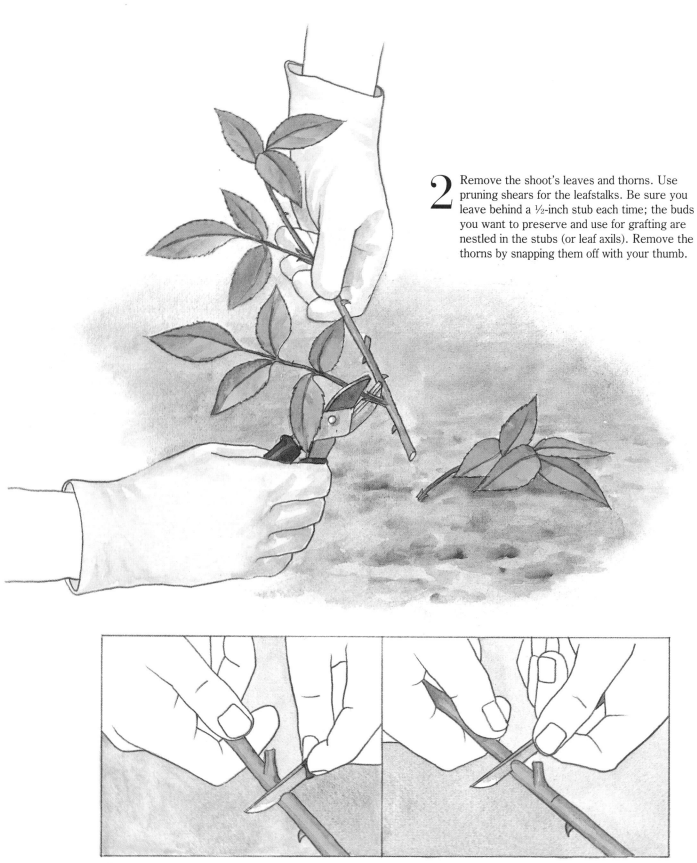

2 Remove the shoot's leaves and thorns. Use pruning shears for the leafstalks. Be sure you leave behind a ½-inch stub each time; the buds you want to preserve and use for grafting are nestled in the stubs (or leaf axils). Remove the thorns by snapping them off with your thumb.

3 Using a small, sharp knife, slice a bud and its surrounding bark—a "bud shield"—from the middle portion of the shoot. Begin by making a horizontal cut about ⅛ inch deep through the bark roughly ½ inch below the bud *(above, left)*. Make an identical cut ½ inch above the bud. Slip the knife blade downward from the top cut *(above, right)* until the knife reaches the bottom cut. You should end with a neat slice of bark with the bud intact.

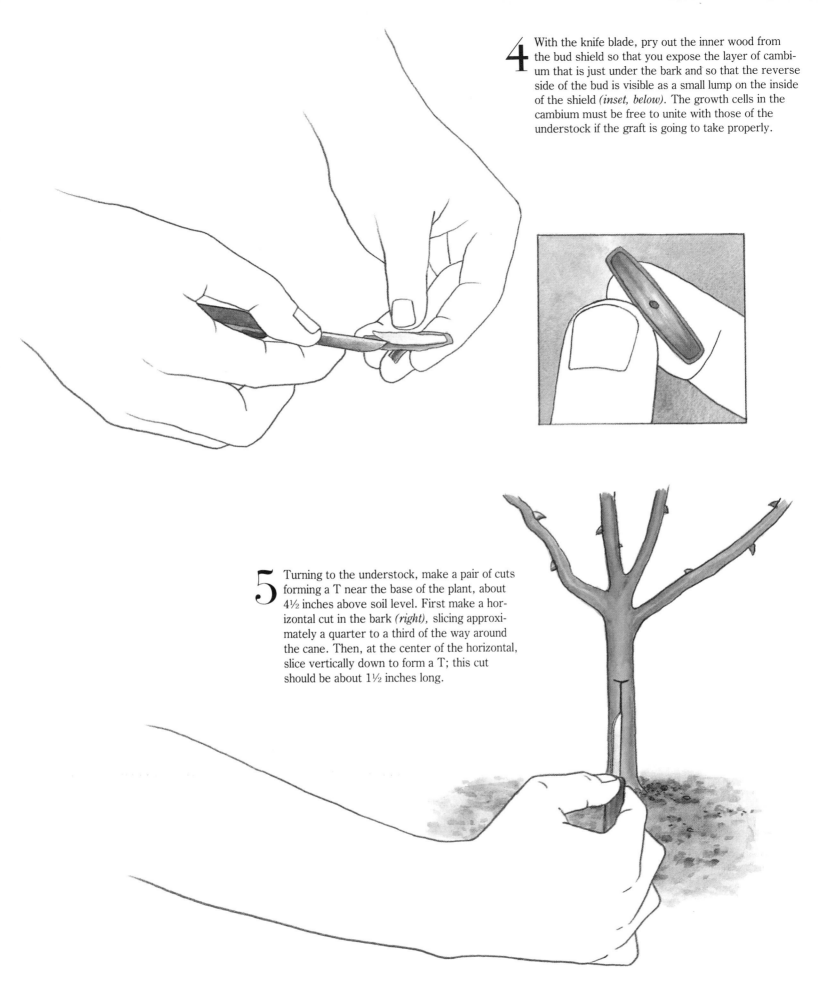

4 With the knife blade, pry out the inner wood from the bud shield so that you expose the layer of cambium that is just under the bark and so that the reverse side of the bud is visible as a small lump on the inside of the shield *(inset, below)*. The growth cells in the cambium must be free to unite with those of the understock if the graft is going to take properly.

5 Turning to the understock, make a pair of cuts forming a T near the base of the plant, about 4½ inches above soil level. First make a horizontal cut in the bark *(right)*, slicing approximately a quarter to a third of the way around the cane. Then, at the center of the horizontal, slice vertically down to form a T; this cut should be about 1½ inches long.

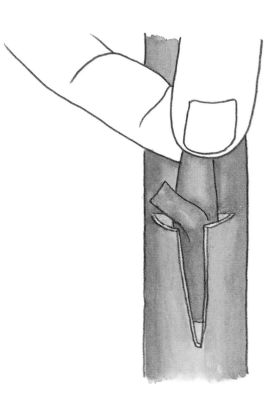

6 With your fingers, bend the corners of the T cut away from the cane to make what amounts to a slot or pocket. Into the slot insert the bud shield *(left)*. The pocket flaps should enclose most of the bark portion of the shield. If any of the bud shield protrudes above the top of the slot, slice off the excess for a snug fit.

7 Secure the graft with a rubber band that has been cut open or with budding tape, a rubber strip that has a hole in the center. Place the tape on the shield so that the hole fits over the stub sheltering the bud, or wrap the band around the shield, in either case leaving the bud exposed, and tie the ends securely.

8 After about three weeks, when the bud has begun to sprout, remove whatever wrapping material you employed—if it has not already disintegrated on its own. Cut the wrapping with a knife on the side of the cane opposite the bud and peel it off. Then cut the top of the rootstock just above the graft *(left)*. □

NEW ROSES
FROM SOFTWOOD STEMS

Roses put out softwood stems at the beginning of each growing season. You can get an exact copy of a rose you admire by cutting a piece from a healthy stem about as thick as a pencil. Properly trimmed and started in a container of sterile medium, it will establish roots within six weeks. Transplanted to a permanent home, the new rose can be expected to reach full maturity after two or three years.

To speed the development of healthy roots, coat the base of each cutting with a commercially available hormone powder before placing it in a container of sterile soilless medium. There are two reasons why such a medium is preferable to ordinary soil: the sterile mix is free of diseases and insect pests, and its loose texture allows fragile young roots to stretch out and grow with minimal resistance.

To sustain the warm, humid conditions that rose cuttings like, enclose the container in a clear plastic bag to create a greenhouse effect. Keep it out of direct sunlight because roses struggling to establish a root system may not survive the heat that will build up.

Once the cutting begins to take root, in three to four weeks, start acclimating it to outdoor conditions. Move the container to a sunny location and open the plastic bag for a few hours. Repeat for progressively longer periods over the next seven to 10 days; then discard the bag and maintain the plant in moist medium for another two weeks until it is fully acclimated. Gently remove it from the container and transfer it to a prepared bed.

A pair of stem cuttings from an 'Olympiad' hybrid tea rose gradually adjust to outdoor conditions in the shade of their parent plant. When mature, the new plants will show the cultivar's long-lasting red flowers with velvety petals.

1 Select a healthy softwood stem that has just finished blooming. Use pruning shears to snip about 7 inches of stem from the parent plant. Make the cut just above a leaf. Since the bloom will only hinder rooting, remove it *(left)*.

2 With your shears, cut off the entire top and bottom leaves; make each cut so that you retain the petiole—the slender stem that supports the leaf and protects the dormant buds. Then cut each of the remaining leaves so that you retain from two to four leaflets. The black bars in the inset indicate the positions for both types of cut.

3 Fill a 4-inch container to within ¾ inch of the rim with sterile soilless growing medium. With a pencil or a stick, poke a hole in the medium to a depth of approximately 1 inch.

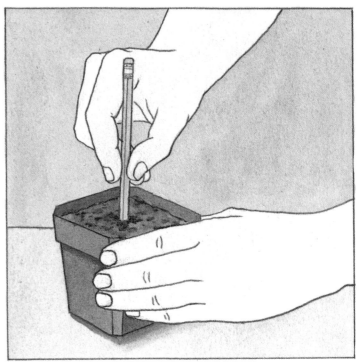

4 Pour a small amount of rooting hormone powder into a plastic bag or onto a paper towel. Wet the base of the stem with water; touch the moistened wood to the powder *(left)* and move the stem back and forth until the base is thoroughly coated.

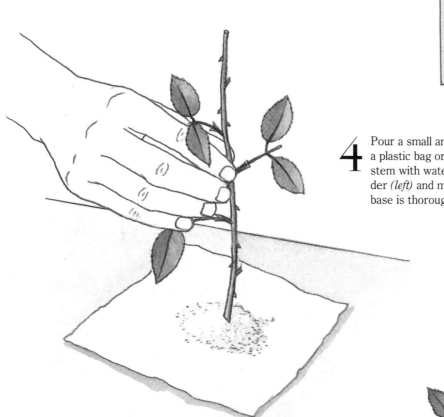

5 Insert the powder-coated base of the stem into the hole and firm the growing medium around the cutting. To water and fertilize at the same time, dilute liquid fertilizer in a watering can to half the recommended strength and thoroughly moisten the medium with the solution.

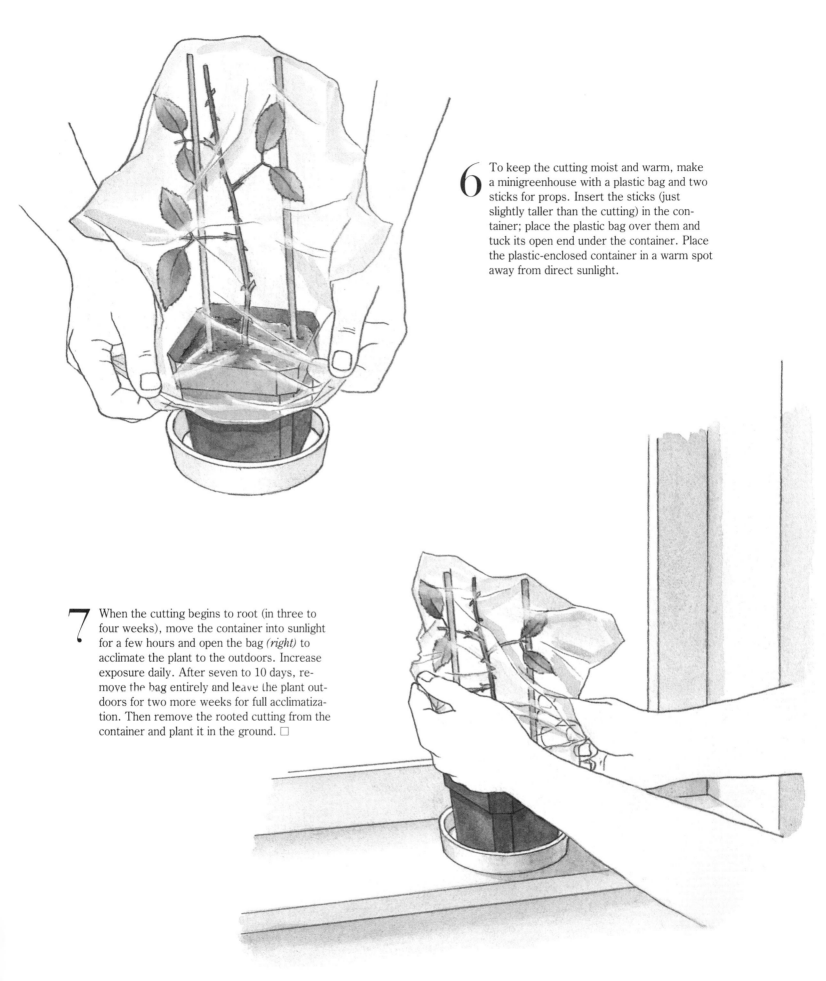

6 To keep the cutting moist and warm, make a minigreenhouse with a plastic bag and two sticks for props. Insert the sticks (just slightly taller than the cutting) in the container; place the plastic bag over them and tuck its open end under the container. Place the plastic-enclosed container in a warm spot away from direct sunlight.

7 When the cutting begins to root (in three to four weeks), move the container into sunlight for a few hours and open the bag (*right*) to acclimate the plant to the outdoors. Increase exposure daily. After seven to 10 days, remove the bag entirely and leave the plant outdoors for two more weeks for full acclimatization. Then remove the rooted cutting from the container and plant it in the ground. □

FROM A BURIED CANE, A VIGOROUS NEW PLANT

The simplest and surest method of propagating old garden roses and climbing roses, which have long and pliable canes, is soil layering, a technique that permits a plant to reproduce itself without grafting or cutting. Soil layering is essentially a three-step process that begins early in the growing season, with the selection of a healthy plant in a sheltered area. A single year-old cane, green, supple and about as thick as a pencil, is stripped of foliage except for its tip. After the bark of the stripped portion is scarred and coated with hormone powder to stimulate root development, the cane is bent to the ground and buried in a shallow trench so that only the tip protrudes.

If the layering is done correctly, and if the buried cane is mulched and kept moist, roots will begin to develop by the end of the growing season. By the beginning of the next season, the cane should be well rooted and ready for the second step of the soil-layering process—severance from the parent plant.

The severed cane, fortified by an application of liquid fertilizer, is then left in place for two or three weeks to adjust to its independence. It will then be safe to proceed with the next step, the removal and transplanting of the new plant to a new location. It is best to remove the plant with a generous root ball to a protected and fertilized interim site for the remainder of the season. The final transfer can then be carried out early in the following season.

An old garden rose, 'Belle de Crecy', bears a profusion of pink blossoms in a raised garden bed. Old garden roses and climbing roses, having long, limber canes, are easily propagated by soil layering—being buried under a thin layer of earth.

1 Select a young, supple cane near the ground and strip it of leaves except for a few inches at the tip. Bend the cane to the ground (*right*) and use a trowel to dig a trench 3 to 4 inches deep and long enough to cover the part of the cane that touches the ground.

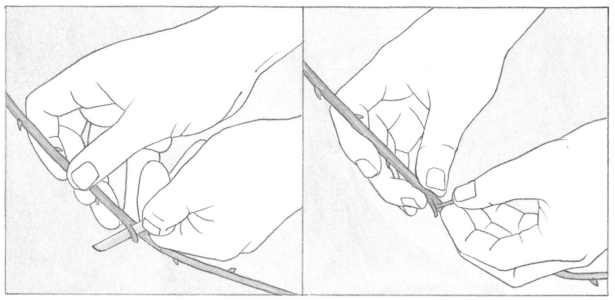

2 At a point where the cane will be buried, and just below a bud, cut a notch *(above, left)* about twice as long as the cane is thick. Wedge the notch open with a bit of wood *(above, right)* and brush hormone powder into the notch to promote root development.

3 Bend the cane into the trench and secure the notched area against the soil with a wood prong *(left)* or with a stone. Refill the trench with the original soil, mixed with enriching compost, but leave the leafy tip protruding and pointing upward. Then mulch the buried portion.

4 Early in the next growing season, sever the rooted cane; cut the cane on the parent just above the point where it disappears into the ground. After two or three weeks, use a trowel to remove the new plant and the soil around the roots. Transplant it into the ground or to a container for further growth before removing it to a permanent site next season. □

TAKING ADVANTAGE OF SUCKERS: AN EASY WAY TO PROPAGATE

During the growing season roses often put forth suckers—those thin shoots that grow straight up from roots. On rose plants that have been grafted, suckers are merely nuisances to be removed as soon as possible, since neither their foliage nor their flowers will resemble the desirable top growth. But roses that grow on their own roots—as do species roses and plants that were started from seed or stem cuttings —produce suckers that share all the characteristics you see in the top growth. These suckers can be easily detached and raised as independent plants.

The ideal time to propagate from such suckers is at the start of the growing season so that the new plants will have ample opportunity to establish themselves before the onset of winter. Choose ones that are growing at some distance from the point at which the rest of the canes emerge. Such outside suckers are younger than interior suckers and tend to be more vigorous. They are also easier to work with, and can be separated from the parent with far less trauma to the main plant and to the prospective new plant.

For best results, try to dig up each sucker with its root system largely intact. Start by loosening the soil around a sucker with a shovel. Then dig down through the loosened soil, severing the sucker's roots from those of the parent. In lifting the sucker, keep as much soil as possible around the roots to prevent them from drying out. Plant the sucker immediately in a container where the roots can recover from the shock of division. Keep the soil moist and feed once a week with diluted liquid fertilizer. In only a few weeks, the new rose plant will be ready to be moved to its permanent home in your garden.

An 'Apothecary's Rose' displays a broad mound of color in a sunny garden location. As an old garden rose that grows on its own roots, it throws up suckers that can be used to start new plants that will have the traits of the parent plant.

1 Look for a vigorous sucker, several inches long, growing approximately 1 foot from the main part of the plant. With the blade of a shovel, loosen a few inches of soil all around the sucker *(right)*.

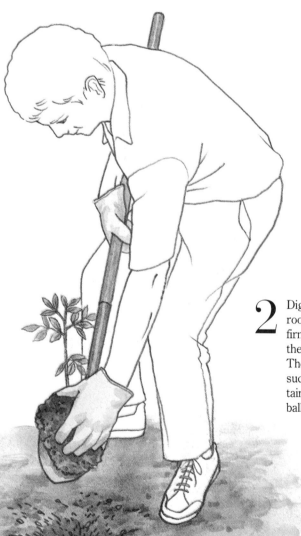

2 Dig down several inches into the root area of the sucker and, with firm thrusts of the shovel, sever the sucker's roots from the parent. Then ease the shovel under the sucker and lift, taking care to retain as much soil around the root ball as possible *(left)*.

3 Partially fill a container with amended soil. Lower the new plant into the container. Add soil to cover the tops of the roots. Firm the soil around the root ball. Apply a diluted solution of liquid fertilizer to the plant once a week. Keep the plant well moistened. After three weeks, transplant it to a prepared bed. □

4
EXTENDED PLEASURES

For as long as there have been roses there have apparently been people dedicated to making these beautiful flowers outperform themselves. There are probably hundreds of precious family formulas for guaranteeing that cut roses will last longer, and the inclusion of roses in the roster of blooms suitable for drying goes back many years. Equally ancient is the use of rose petals as an ingredient in potpourris, those delightful assemblages of blossoms and spices that have perfumed all manner of household interiors from medieval castles to modern condominiums. And everywhere in the modern world, rosarians, those specialized gardeners who make a cult of rose growing, annually cosset and coddle their plants in order to produce the perfect blooms that win prizes at flower shows.

In the section that follows are contemporary recipes and formulas for extending the decorative life of roses as cut flowers, dried flowers and potpourris. Although they are based on the best scientific evidence, they are not without a touch of the secret-ingredient syndrome. A splash of citric-flavored soft drink in the water of a rose bouquet is, for example, a recommended deterrent to decay. And a splash of brandy or vodka will do wonders to revive the fading scent of a potpourri.

Finally, to round out this section on tinkering, there is an introduction to the rituals of rosarians. Beginning weeks before show time, they embark on a series of tactics designed to bring out the best qualities in one particular rose. The qualities have been given numerical values, and the perfect rose will have a score of 100, based on such criteria as form, color, size, substance, proportions, and the condition of leaves and stems. Few weekend gardeners are likely to care this much about evaluating even their most beloved rose, but the techniques used to achieve these splendid blooms are applicable to any rose—even one bought at a supermarket.

CUTTING BLOOMS AND KEEPING THEM BRIGHT

Cutting roses for indoor bouquets takes delicate care. It has to be done in the right way and at the right time—and with a touch of artistic flair as well. First, there is the matter of timing. With many varieties, roses can be cut any time during the growing season. In fact, taking a bloom here and there can, like judicious pruning, rejuvenate the plant. With repeat-blooming varieties, it can also encourage new flowering shoots to develop. However, snipping late in the season is a bad idea. The blossoms of repeat bloomers start to produce seeds a month or so before the first hard frost. Seed production slows the plants' metabolism, preparing them for winter dormancy. Cutting late blooms upsets their seasonal rhythm.

Then there is the time of day. Roses are best cut late in the afternoon, probably because at that hour the blooms contain a full ration of the natural sugars the plant has created during the day.

The flower itself should be just opening, and its sepals—the leaflike coverings of the rosebuds—should have unfurled. Cut earlier, a bud may not open up properly; later, the bloom will be past its prime. The snipping should be done with clean, sharp pruning shears, to minimize tissue damage and prevent spreading disease. Keep the length of the cut stem in proportion to the flower. There is no point in taking extra stem, because the foliage produces nutrients and distributes them throughout the plant. The loss of too much foliage will weaken the rose plant.

Once cut, the blooms should be put in water immediately and the stem should be further cut underwater, to seal off air that would be drawn through the stem and make the flower wilt and die. The water in the vase in which they will stand needs a preservative consisting of sugar to nourish the flower and a disinfectant to kill bacteria. You can either combine table sugar with household bleach or use a soft drink containing both sugar and citric acid, as shown opposite.

A bouquet of roses in an array of hues—rose, red, mauve, salmon and yellow—makes a spectacular display in a Victorian cut-glass rose bowl. Gathered from a garden when the buds are just beginning to open and carefully prepared, such blossoms can remain showy for a week.

1 After selecting a just-opening bloom, cut the stem below it with shears at a 45° angle about ¼ inch above an outside leaf. With repeat-blooming roses, snip above a pair of five-leaflet leaves. The buds in these leaf axils will grow the strongest flowering stems.

2 To help preserve the flower, quickly plunge its stem into water heated to about 110° F. Then, while the stem is still in the water, make a fresh cut in its base, taking off about ¼ inch. Leave the stem submerged for 30 minutes to make sure that the water arrests the flow of air to the blossom.

3 After a half hour, take your cutting from the water and remove any leaves from the lower two-thirds of the stem with your fingers (using a knife could harm the stem). Fill a vase with a quart or so of ordinary water, and add a preservative: either two teaspoons of sugar plus a few drops of bleach, or two teaspoons of a soft drink that contains both sugar and citric acid. Place the rose and the vase in a cool, dark room for a few hours to let the bloom adjust before displaying it. Renew the water every day—cut roses need a lot—each time adding the preservative. □

DRYING ROSES FOR ENDURING BEAUTY

The evanescent grandeur of a perfect rose, a vision all too brief in nature, can be preserved and enjoyed between growing seasons by a simple process of air drying, a technique of removing moisture from cut flowers. Although the colors undergo subtle changes—red roses take on deeper shades; pink and yellow roses fade slightly and assume more muted tones—the petals remain intact and unwithered, and the roses provide lifelike mementos that delight the eye and lend elegance to indoor floral arrangements, especially when tastefully combined with the contrasting shapes and colors of other dried flowers.

Roses selected for preservation should be flawless specimens. They should be cut before they are fully opened and preferably in the morning, after the dew has dried. Although they can be dried individually, it is more practical to combine about five into a bouquet, with the flower heads separated to permit the free circulation of air around them.

Several such bouquets can be dried simultaneously by suspending them upside down, at least 1 foot apart, from the ceiling of a warm, dry, unlighted room or a closet. Within three weeks, after all their moisture has evaporated, the dried flowers will be ready for display.

When displayed, as when drying, the roses need to be kept in a dry and well-ventilated area; ironically, the moisture and sunlight that nurtured them in life are their greatest threats in a state of preservation. Excessive humidity can produce mold, and direct sunlight tends to bleach the remaining colors.

Handsome bouquets of drying roses, their partly opened flowers retaining the elegant shapes and pastel tones they possessed in life, hang from an attic rafter. When fully dried, such roses can provide striking indoor displays for months and even years.

1 Select several well-formed, half-opened roses and cut them with about 6 inches of stem after the morning dew has evaporated. Remove the leaves from the lower stem of each flower, retaining only small leaves near the top of the stem.

2 Bunch the stems so that the flower heads are staggered. Tie the stem ends together by twisting a loop of plastic-covered garden wire around them. Cut off about 8 inches of wire beyond the loop.

3 Form a loop at the other end of the wire and hang the bouquet upside down from a small hook or a nail in the ceiling of a warm, dry, unlighted room or the top of a closed cupboard. After about three weeks, when the dried leaves and petals are stiff to the touch, the bouquet will be ready for display. □

A ROSE-BASED POTPOURRI FOR LONG-LASTING AROMA

Ever since ancient times, people have sought to preserve the ravishing fragrance of roses in bloom. In Egypt, decaying rose petals were stored in jars and used to scent the households of kings and queens. The 18th-century English adopted and improved the method, and the French provided a word for it: *potpourri* (literally "rotten pot").

Modern potpourri—which uses dried petals that won't rot—is easy to make. After drying, the petals are sealed in a container along with herbs, spices, fragrant oils and a fixative. When opened after six weeks, this concoction makes a natural air sweetener for drawers, closets, even entire rooms.

Start your potpourri with some fragrant variety of rose, such as an old garden rose or one of the hybrid teas or floribundas. Add other flowers, such as lavender, for a richer, more complex perfume. Try to pick newly opened blossoms just after the morning dew has vanished; they will contain more of the essential aromatic oils.

The container is important. You can use metal containers for short-term displays, but not for storing; over time metal reacts with substances in the petals to destroy fragrance. To enjoy the colorful display of the dried petals, store the potpourri in a glass jar. If the jar has a metal lid, line the lid and cover the mouth of the jar with plastic. Potpourri can also be made and stored in enameled pots.

If the potpourri loses its sweet scent after many months, don't throw it out. Simply reactivate the fragrance by adding a few drops of brandy or vodka and covering the jar for a few days.

Dried rosebuds and petals mingle with herbal leaves to make a cheerful display in a silver dish whose delicate filigree enables the fragrances to pass through and scent the surrounding air.

1 After gathering fresh rose blossoms, pick off the petals and spread them out on a screen or a drying rack. Don't let the petals touch one another. Leave the screen in a warm, dry place, out of direct sunlight. The petals should be dry within a few days. Separately, dry a few whole rosebuds, some lavender, some rosemary and some orange peel.

2 In a bowl, combine 1 cup of dried rose petals, ½ cup of dried lavender and ¼ cup of dried rosemary. Add ⅛ teaspoon of ground cloves and ground cinnamon, plus a few dried rosebuds and pieces of orange peel. Toss the mixture as you would a salad. Add a few drops of oil of rose or oil of lavender and toss again. Add ¼ teaspoon of some fixative, such as crushed orris root. Mix well.

3 Pour the mixture through a funnel into a glass jar *(left)* or into a ceramic bowl or an enameled one. If the jar has a metal lid, line the lid and cover the mouth of the jar with plastic wrap. Store the container in a cool dark place for six weeks.

4 Within six weeks, the scents should have blended together and the potpourri should be moist. Transfer it to an open bowl or to a container with a tight-fitting lid that can be removed whenever you want to release the fragrance. Or sew the mixture inside little cloth bags to make attractive sachets for drawers, closet shelves and storage boxes. □

EXHIBITION-QUALITY BLOOMS AND HOW THEY ARE JUDGED

Typically, growers of roses start with a few plants—only to find themselves collecting dozens. Before long, many enthusiasts move on to another step: cultivating exhibition-quality blooms. Striving for the ideal rose often proves the most potent fascination of all. Those who succumb may end up exhibiting their best blooms in rose shows. The competition can be rewarding, even exhilarating. Also, going to exhibitions gives a grower the chance to see what class A, show-worthy blossoms are like. Hundreds of shows are held each year at local, regional and national levels.

An interested beginner should contact a nearby rose society about joining, and visit several shows before taking on the challenge of entering one. Veteran exhibitors will be happy to discuss their entries, and to share hints about growing topflight roses. They can also provide more information about shows held around the country and names and addresses of the nationwide network of expert rosarians.

The criteria for telling whether a rose meets exhibition standards are explained here and on the next two pages. The illustrations on the facing page show the three blossom types normally exhibited. On the following two pages are the guidelines show judges use when awarding prizes. Most important in any bloom are its shape or form and its color. Then the judges consider what they call substance—the petals' freshness and sheen—as well as stem and foliage, overall balance and proportion, and a bloom's size. The drawings should be interesting even to rose growers who never intend to exhibit but would like to know how close their best blooms are to prizewinning perfection.

The smooth, shapely petals of a pink and yellow 'Granada' rose gleam above a strong, straight stem. Evenly shaded coloring, symmetrical form and spiraling flower centers are characteristic of prizewinning roses.

FORMAL

Of the three sorts of blooms shown on this page, the variety at right—called exhibition form or (redundantly) formal form—is the most complex. A formal blossom should have a roughly circular and symmetrical arrangement of 25 to 50 petals. The center should be pointed and higher than the petals around it. This sort of blossom *must* be one-half to two-thirds open when exhibited so the judges can see inside the tight-furled outer petals and be sure the center is also well shaped.

DECORATIVE

Also called an informal blossom, a decorative is more open than a formal bloom, but it is also a double flower with distinct inner and outer ranges of 25 to 50 petals. The center is not raised in the same way, but rather can be flat or even somewhat sunken in appearance; rose growers call this form cup-shaped.

SINGLE

Unlike the other blossom types pictured here, this simple sort of rose has a single tier of petals—and there are only five to a dozen of them. The petals surround a center cluster of stamens, which should be fresh, and be pure and bright in color.

ONE BLOSSOM PER STEM: SIGNS OF PERFECTION

Roses are exhibited in two configurations—with one blossom topping a stem or with a spray of blooms growing from one main stem. The one-blossom type is pictured below, with captions outlining the qualities a judge at a rose show would look for in a solo bloom and in its stem and leaves. Judges award various numbers of points (totaling 100) for the different qualities and consider the same marks of excellence whether the rose is a hybrid tea, floribunda, grandiflora or miniature.

COLOR

The color of a blossom should be pure, bright and even—that is, no streaks on the petals—as well as typical of the variety of rose. Color is worth a maximum of 20 points.

SUBSTANCE

All petals should be firm and crisp, and have a soft sheen—sure signs that the bloom received adequate moisture before being cut and shown. Substance merits 15 points.

FLOWER FORM

The blossom's shape should be graceful, balanced and ideal for the cultivar. Form is worth the highest number of points, 25.

SIZE

Judges consider size last but it is still important. A bloom must be at least as large as the normal for its variety. An average-sized blossom usually receives 7 points; another 3 go to glorious outsized blooms for a possible total of 10.

BALANCE AND PROPORTION

Blossom, foliage and stem ought to be in harmony with one another. A large bloom needs a long stem and abundant leaves. A smaller flower looks best with a shorter stem and sparser foliage. Balance and proportion are worth 10 points.

STEM AND FOLIAGE

Judges look for a straight stem that is strong enough to support the bloom. The leaves ought to be clean, have clear color and make a neat pattern. Together these qualities fetch 20 points.

SPRAYS OF BLOSSOMS: SOME ADDED REQUIREMENTS

The main qualities—blossom shape and substance —that judges value in roses borne singly are also important for roses borne in clusters. But with sprays judges have a few extra criteria, including of course the overall form and proportion of the cluster. Then there are a few special rules, most notably that clusters cut from floribundas and miniatures need to include flowers at several stages of maturity *(below)*.

DEVELOPMENT

Sprays from some cultivars should include blooms at several degrees of openness—a bud or two, some blooms one-fourth open, some at normal exhibition stage and a couple fully opened with stamens showing. Exception: the blossoms in grandiflora clusters must all be one-half or two-thirds open.

CLUSTER FORM

The blossoms in a spray should be well formed themselves, but their arrangement also counts. Ideally, they should be evenly spaced and give an overall impression of symmetry and balance.

PROPORTION OF STEM AND BLOOM

Clusters of blooms will naturally be larger in proportion to their main stem than blossoms borne singly. Still, the stem ought to be strong enough to support the spray, and its foliage should complement and embellish the whole effect. □

READYING ROSES FOR A SHOW

Many rose growers who find they have bushes that produce show-quality blooms succumb to the urge to show off their triumphs. And they certainly should: entering rose exhibitions can be great fun and a fine way to meet other enthusiasts. The best way to prepare is, first, to talk to a fellow rosarian and find out about the local rose society's shows. Then attend one or two of them, to see what exhibiting involves. Be sure to obtain a schedule of the season's shows and read the rules that participants will be asked to follow.

Having collected this information, begin pampering the show-level rosebush so that it will grow with extra vigor and produce its best blooms. About six weeks or so before a show, prune back the canes halfway to force new growth. Three weeks before the show, start giving the bush extra moisture—at least two deep waterings a week. Stop spraying with insecticides when the buds appear; sprays can damage the petals. As promising buds begin to open, protect them from heavy rain, insects and other perils with plastic sandwich bags. Twist ties loosely around the bottom of bag and stem. The buds should stay covered until they have reached exhibition stage—one-half to two-thirds open.

The proper way to cut a rose is described on pages 74-75. The best time to cut depends on the variety. Ideally, the flower selected should reach exhibition stage the morning of the show.

The length of the cut stem should, of course, be in proportion to the size of the blossom; the bigger the flower, the longer the stem. Finally, groom the rose before taking it to the show. How to make these last preparations is shown at right and on the opposite page. It is also a good idea to take some cotton swabs and pruning shears to the show for last-minute touch-ups.

An array of floribundas with one bloom per stem display their prizewinning shapes and colors at a flower show. Anyone who produces a spectacular rose is free to enter a rose show; the only requirement is that the entry be registered with the show authorities.

1 On the morning of the rose show, cut the flower you have decided to exhibit. Clean the leaves with a moist, soft cloth and remove any mildew with a mild mixture of water and baking soda. Then polish the leaves with a dry cloth. Do not shine the foliage with oil or petroleum jelly.

2 Remove any damaged petals by wiggling them gently back and forth with your fingers until they loosen at the base and snap off. The same goes for any outside petals *(left)* that seem to spoil the blossom's symmetry.

3 Remove the bottom leaves from the stem with your fingers *(right)*. Write the name of the rose cultivar on an adhesive label and attach it to the container you will use to take the rose to the show.

4 Fill the jar with water and put the rose in it. Set the jar in a box, stuffing newspaper around it to prevent tipping. If you are exhibiting more than one rose, use separate containers and be sure the blooms do not jostle one another. At the show, fill out the official entry tag that will identify your rose, and do some final grooming. □

5
MAKING THE MOST OF NATURE

For roses to succeed they need a helping hand, a willing heart and what may seem at times like constant attention. In fact, with a little intelligent planning, many of the traditional problems of rose culture can be bypassed or simplified. Winter cold, for example, will be easier to deal with if the rose variety is suited to the zone in which it is to be planted; the zone map on pages 88-89 will clarify this correlation. Using the same map in conjunction with the checklist of chores on pages 90-93, rose gardeners can fit their seasonal activities to local climate conditions. Thus, in January and February in Zone 8, gardeners can safely begin to set out bare-root roses, while gardeners living in Zone 6 must for the moment be content with studying rose catalogs and sharpening their tools. Intelligent planning can also minimize the problems of pests and diseases; using the information in the chart on pages 94-97 may help you beat trouble before it starts.

As a postscript to these necessary chores, a series of tips and techniques suggests ways in which the pleasure of roses can be expanded or improved. There are proposals for using rose hips, for adapting roses to use as ground cover, for preventing pot-grown roses from drying out, for speeding growth in bare-root plants and for interplanting roses with other types of plants to provide color when the roses are dormant. Finally, for sentimentalists who want mementos of their roses long after the roses themselves have ceased to be, there are tips for photographing roses at the moment when they are most photogenic.

THE ZONE MAP AND PLANTING

Practically all roses grow well in warm climates. In moderately cold climates, some roses need a protective covering of mulch or soil during winter. In the very cold climates of the northernmost part of the United States, all roses need winter protection.

The zone map on the right can help you determine how cold your winter climate is and thus which types of roses need protection in it. The map has been prepared by the U.S. Department of Agriculture, and it divides North America into 10 climatic zones based on average minimum winter temperatures. Zone 1 is the coldest; winter temperatures are as low as −50° F. Zone 10 is the warmest; winter temperatures drop no lower than 30° to 40° F. These temperatures should be used only as guidelines. Because they are averages compiled over many years, they may vary by several degrees in any given year.

In Zones 9 and 10, which are generally frost-free, roses can survive without winter protection. In Zone 8, tender roses need protection during spells of unusual winter cold. In Zones 1 through 7, tender roses need protection throughout the winter season.

In Zones 1 through 6, semihardy roses need protection. In Zones 1 through 5, hardy roses require protection. In the coldest areas, Zones 1 through 4, all roses, including those that are extremely hardy, need protection.

If you live in an area with heavy snowfalls, it is possible to grow roses in temperatures slightly colder than those recommended, because snow is an excellent insulator against cold.

For information about the hardiness of specific roses, consult the Dictionary of Roses *(pages 100-151)*. Once you determine that the roses you grow need protection in your area, you can use the monthly maintenance chart on the following pages to determine when winter protection should be applied.

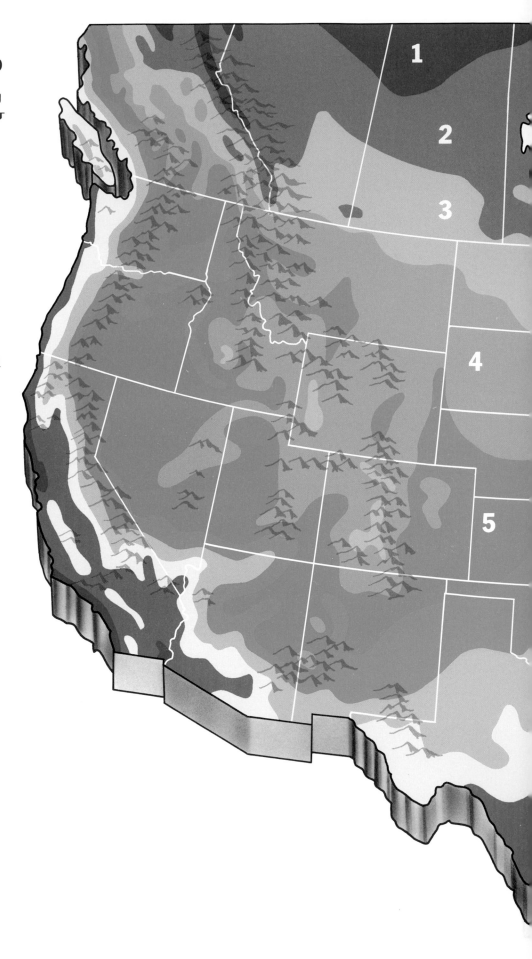

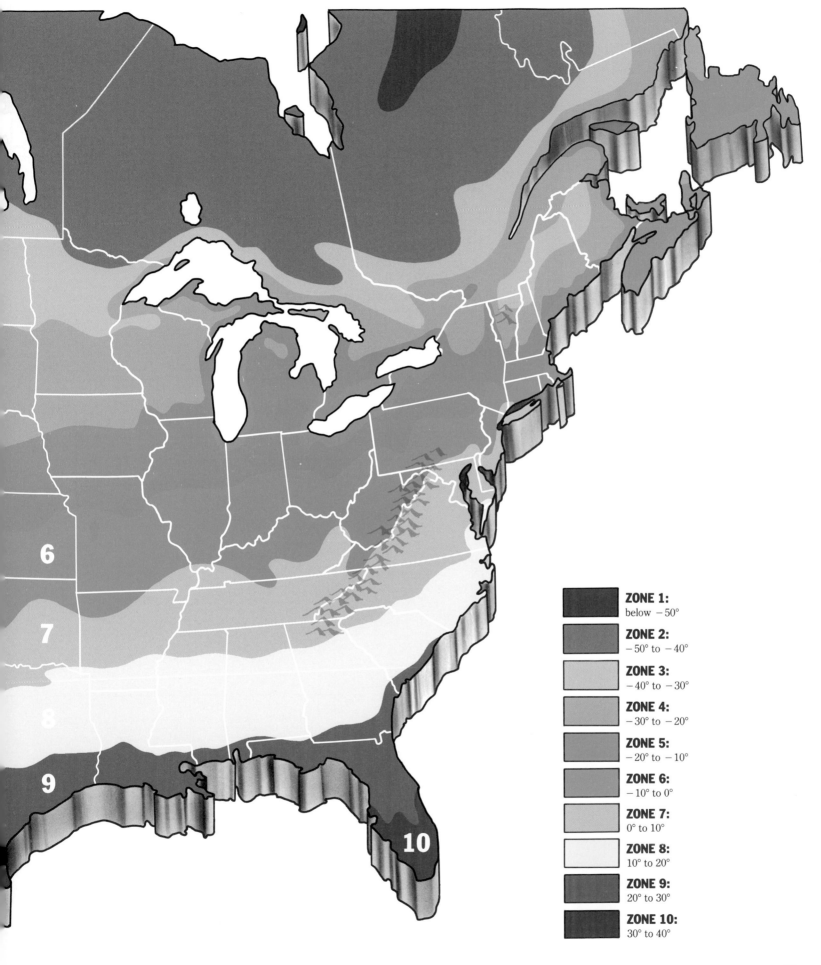

	ZONE 1: below −50°
	ZONE 2: −50° to −40°
	ZONE 3: −40° to −30°
	ZONE 4: −30° to −20°
	ZONE 5: −20° to −10°
	ZONE 6: −10° to 0°
	ZONE 7: 0° to 10°
	ZONE 8: 10° to 20°
	ZONE 9: 20° to 30°
	ZONE 10: 30° to 40°

A CHECKLIST FOR MAINTENANCE MONTH BY MONTH

	ZONE 1	ZONE 2	ZONE 3	ZONE 4	ZONE 5
JANUARY/FEBRUARY	• Read catalogs; order roses for spring planting • Clean, oil, sharpen tools	• Read catalogs; order roses for spring planting • Clean, oil, sharpen tools	• Read catalogs; order roses for spring planting • Clean, oil, sharpen tools	• Read catalogs; order roses for spring planting • Clean, oil, sharpen tools	• Read catalogs; order roses for spring planting • Clean, oil, sharpen tools
MARCH/APRIL	• Test soil pH; adjust if necessary • Plant bare-root roses • Plant container-grown roses • Transplant any roses that need to be moved • Remove winter protection • Begin pruning in mid-April • Apply granular fertilizer after pruning • Water as necessary	• Test soil pH; adjust if necessary • Plant bare-root roses • Plant container-grown roses • Transplant any roses that need to be moved • Remove winter protection • Begin pruning in mid-April • Apply granular fertilizer after pruning • Water as necessary	• Test soil pH; adjust if necessary • Plant bare-root roses • Plant container-grown roses • Transplant any roses that need to be moved • Remove winter protection • Begin pruning in mid-April • Apply granular fertilizer after pruning • Water as necessary	• Test soil pH; adjust if necessary • Plant bare-root roses • Plant container-grown roses • Transplant any roses that need to be moved • Remove winter protection • Begin pruning in mid-April • Apply granular fertilizer after pruning • Water as necessary	• Test soil pH; adjust if necessary • Plant bare-root roses • Plant container-grown roses • Transplant any roses that need to be moved • Remove winter protection • Begin pruning in mid-April • Apply granular fertilizer after pruning • Water as necessary
MAY/JUNE	• Plant container-grown roses • Remove side buds to encourage large single blossoms, or remove terminal buds to encourage clusters of blossoms • Deadhead faded flowers • Apply granular fertilizer • Apply supplemental liquid fertilizer • Weed soil • Begin spraying regularly with a fungicide • Apply mulch for summer • Water as necessary	• Plant container-grown roses • Remove side buds to encourage large single blossoms, or remove terminal buds to encourage clusters of blossoms • Deadhead faded flowers • Apply granular fertilizer • Apply supplemental liquid fertilizer • Weed soil • Begin spraying regularly with a fungicide • Apply mulch for summer • Water as necessary	• Plant container-grown roses • Remove side buds to encourage large single blossoms, or remove terminal buds to encourage clusters of blossoms • Deadhead faded flowers • Apply granular fertilizer • Apply supplemental liquid fertilizer • Weed soil • Begin spraying regularly with a fungicide • Apply mulch for summer • Water as necessary	• Plant container-grown roses • Remove side buds to encourage large single blossoms, or remove terminal buds to encourage clusters of blossoms • Deadhead faded flowers • Apply granular fertilizer • Apply supplemental liquid fertilizer • Weed soil • Begin spraying regularly with a fungicide • Apply mulch for summer • Water as necessary	• Plant container-grown roses • Remove side buds to encourage large single blossoms, or remove terminal buds to encourage clusters of blossoms • Deadhead faded flowers • Apply granular fertilizer • Apply supplemental liquid fertilizer • Weed soil • Begin spraying regularly with a fungicide • Apply mulch for summer • Water as necessary

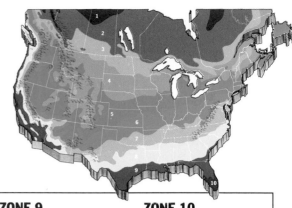

	ZONE 6	ZONE 7	ZONE 8	ZONE 9	ZONE 10	
	• Read catalogs; order roses for spring planting • Clean, oil, sharpen tools	• Read catalogs; order roses for spring planting • Clean, oil, sharpen tools	• Test soil pH; adjust if necessary • Plant bare-root roses • Plant container-grown roses • Transplant any roses that need to be moved • Begin pruning in mid-February • Apply granular fertilizer after pruning • Resume watering	• Test soil pH; adjust if necessary • Plant bare-root roses • Plant container-grown roses • Transplant any roses that need to be moved • Begin pruning in mid-February • Apply granular fertilizer after pruning • Resume watering	• Test soil pH; adjust if necessary • Plant bare-root roses • Plant container-grown roses • Transplant any roses that need to be moved • Begin pruning in late January • Apply granular fertilizer after pruning • Resume watering	**JANUARY/FEBRUARY**
	• Test soil pH; adjust if necessary • Plant bare-root roses • Plant container-grown roses • Transplant any roses that need to be moved • Remove winter protection • Begin pruning in early April • Apply granular fertilizer after pruning • Water as necessary	• Test soil pH; adjust if necessary • Plant bare-root roses • Plant container-grown roses • Transplant any roses that need to be moved • Remove winter protection • Begin pruning in late March • Apply granular fertilizer after pruning • Weed soil • Water as necessary	• Plant container-grown roses • Remove side buds to encourage large single blossoms, or remove terminal buds to encourage clusters of blossoms • Deadhead faded flowers • Apply granular fertilizer • Apply supplemental liquid fertilizer • Begin spraying regularly with a fungicide • Weed soil • Apply mulch for summer • Water as necessary	• Plant container-grown roses • Remove side buds to encourage large single blossoms, or remove terminal buds to encourage clusters of blossoms • Deadhead faded flowers • Apply granular fertilizer • Apply supplemental liquid fertilizer • Weed soil • Begin spraying regularly with a fungicide • Apply mulch for summer • Water as necessary	• Plant container-grown roses • Remove side buds to encourage large single blossoms, or remove terminal buds to encourage clusters of blossoms • Deadhead faded flowers • Apply granular fertilizer • Apply supplemental liquid fertilizer • Weed soil • Begin spraying regularly with a fungicide • Apply mulch for summer • Water as necessary	**MARCH/APRIL**
	• Plant container-grown roses • Remove side buds to encourage large single blossoms, or remove terminal buds to encourage clusters of blossoms • Deadhead faded flowers • Apply granular fertilizer • Apply supplemental liquid fertilizer • Weed soil • Begin spraying regularly with a fungicide • Apply mulch for summer • Water as necessary	• Plant container-grown roses • Remove side buds to encourage large single blossoms, or remove terminal buds to encourage clusters of blossoms • Deadhead faded flowers • Apply granular fertilizer • Apply supplemental liquid fertilizer • Weed soil • Begin spraying regularly with a fungicide • Apply mulch for summer • Water as necessary	• Plant container-grown roses • Remove side buds to encourage large single blossoms, or remove terminal buds to encourage clusters of blossoms • Deadhead faded flowers • Apply granular fertilizer • Apply supplemental liquid fertilizer • Weed soil • Water as necessary	• Plant container-grown roses • Remove side buds to encourage large single blossoms, or remove terminal buds to encourage clusters of blossoms • Deadhead faded flowers • Apply granular fertilizer • Apply supplemental liquid fertilizer • Weed soil • Continue spraying regularly with a fungicide • Water as necessary	• Plant container-grown roses • Remove side buds to encourage large single blossoms, or remove terminal buds to encourage clusters of blossoms • Deadhead faded flowers • Apply granular fertilizer • Apply supplemental liquid fertilizer • Weed soil • Continue spraying regularly with a fungicide • Water as necessary	**MAY/JUNE**

	ZONE 1	ZONE 2	ZONE 3	ZONE 4	ZONE 5
JULY/AUGUST	• Plant container-grown roses • Remove side buds to encourage large single blossoms, or remove terminal buds to encourage clusters of blossoms • Deadhead faded flowers • Apply granular fertilizer until mid-August • Apply supplemental liquid fertilizer until mid-August • Weed soil • Continue spraying regularly with a fungicide • Water as necessary	• Plant container-grown roses • Remove side buds to encourage large single blossoms, or remove terminal buds to encourage clusters of blossoms • Deadhead faded flowers • Apply granular fertilizer until mid-August • Apply supplemental liquid fertilizer until mid-August • Weed soil • Continue spraying regularly with a fungicide • Water as necessary	• Plant container-grown roses • Remove side buds to encourage large single blossoms, or remove terminal buds to encourage clusters of blossoms • Deadhead faded flowers • Apply granular fertilizer until mid-August • Apply supplemental liquid fertilizer until mid-August • Weed soil • Continue spraying regularly with a fungicide • Water as necessary	• Plant container-grown roses • Remove side buds to encourage large single blossoms, or remove terminal buds to encourage clusters of blossoms • Deadhead faded flowers • Apply granular fertilizer until mid-August • Apply supplemental liquid fertilizer until mid-August • Weed soil • Continue spraying regularly with a fungicide • Water as necessary	• Plant container-grown roses • Remove side buds to encourage large single blossoms, or remove terminal buds to encourage clusters of blossoms • Deadhead faded flowers • Apply granular fertilizer until mid-August • Apply supplemental liquid fertilizer until mid-August • Weed soil • Continue spraying regularly with a fungicide • Water as necessary
SEPTEMBER/OCTOBER	• Discontinue deadheading in early September • Discontinue watering in early October • Prepare soil for spring planting • Apply winter protection in October	• Discontinue deadheading in early September • Discontinue watering in early October • Prepare soil for spring planting • Apply winter protection in October	• Discontinue deadheading in early September • Discontinue watering in early October • Prepare soil for spring planting • Apply winter protection in October	• Discontinue deadheading in early September • Discontinue watering in early October • Prepare soil for spring planting • Apply winter protection in October	• Discontinue deadheading in early September • Transplant any roses that need to be moved • Discontinue watering in mid-October • Weed soil • Prepare soil for spring planting
NOVEMBER/DECEMBER					• Apply winter protection in November

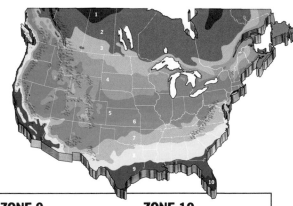

	ZONE 6	ZONE 7	ZONE 8	ZONE 9	ZONE 10	
	• Plant container-grown roses • Remove side buds to encourage large single blossoms, or remove terminal buds to encourage clusters of blossoms • Deadhead faded flowers • Apply granular fertilizer until mid-August • Apply supplemental liquid fertilizer until mid-August • Weed soil • Continue spraying regularly with a fungicide • Water as necessary	• Plant container-grown roses • Remove side buds to encourage large single blossoms, or remove terminal buds to encourage clusters of blossoms • Deadhead faded flowers • Apply granular fertilizer until mid-August • Apply supplemental liquid fertilizer until mid-August • Weed soil • Continue spraying regularly with a fungicide • Water as necessary	• Plant container-grown roses • Remove side buds to encourage large single blossoms, or remove terminal buds to encourage clusters of blossoms • Deadhead faded flowers • Apply granular fertilizer • Apply supplemental liquid fertilizer • Weed soil • Continue spraying regularly with a fungicide • Water as necessary	• Plant container-grown roses • Remove side buds to encourage large single blossoms, or remove terminal buds to encourage clusters of blossoms • Deadhead faded flowers • Apply granular fertilizer • Apply supplemental liquid fertilizer • Weed soil • Continue spraying regularly with a fungicide • Water as necessary	• Plant container-grown roses • Remove side buds to encourage large single blossoms, or remove terminal buds to encourage clusters of blossoms • Deadhead faded flowers • Apply granular fertilizer • Apply supplemental liquid fertilizer • Weed soil • Continue spraying regularly with a fungicide • Water as necessary	**JULY/AUGUST**
	• Discontinue deadheading in mid-September • Discontinue watering in mid-October • Weed soil • Read catalogs; order roses for late-fall planting	• Plant container-grown roses • Continue spraying regularly with a fungicide • Discontinue deadheading in early October • Discontinue watering in mid-October • Weed soil • Read catalogs; order roses for late-fall planting	• Plant container-grown roses • Apply granular fertilizer until early September • Continue spraying regularly with a fungicide • Discontinue deadheading in early October • Discontinue watering in mid-October • Weed soil • Read catalogs; order roses for late-fall planting	• Plant container-grown roses • Apply granular fertilizer until early September • Continue spraying regularly with a fungicide • Discontinue deadheading in mid-October • Discontinue watering in mid-October • Weed soil • Read catalogs: order roses for late-fall planting	• Plant container-grown roses • Apply granular fertilizer until early September • Continue spraying regularly with a fungicide • Discontinue deadheading in mid-October • Discontinue watering in mid-October • Weed soil • Read catalogs; order roses for late-fall planting	**SEPTEMBER/OCTOBER**
	• Plant bare-root roses • Transplant any roses that need to be moved • Prepare soil for spring planting • Apply winter protection in November	• Plant bare-root roses • Transplant any roses that need to be moved • Prepare soil for spring planting • Apply winter protection in November	• Plant bare-root roses • Plant container-grown roses • Transplant any roses that need to be moved • Prepare soil for spring planting • Read catalogs; order roses for spring planting • Clean, oil, sharpen tools	• Plant bare-root roses • Plant container-grown roses • Transplant any roses that need to be moved • Prepare soil for spring planting • Read catalogs; order roses for spring planting • Clean, oil, sharpen tools	• Plant bare-root roses • Plant container-grown roses • Transplant any roses that need to be moved • Prepare soil for spring planting • Read catalogs; order roses for spring planting • Clean, oil, sharpen tools	**NOVEMBER/DECEMBER**

WHAT TO DO
WHEN THINGS GO WRONG

PROBLEM	CAUSE	SOLUTION
Circular black spots ¼ inch in diameter appear on upper leaf surfaces. Each black spot is surrounded by a yellow halo. As the spots enlarge and coalesce, the entire leaf turns yellow and falls from the plant.	Black spot, a fungus disease. The disease is most common in humid and rainy conditions; the fungus spores germinate in water. Once a plant is infected, the fungus will remain in the canes through the winter and reappear on the next season's growth.	There is no chemical cure for infected plants. In the early spring, after an infection, prune the canes back lower than normal to eliminate fungus spores that remained on the canes over winter, and apply a lime-sulfur spray before the leaves open. To prevent black spot from infecting new plants, spray with a synthetic chemical fungicide once every 10 days, starting in midspring. If symptoms appear, remove and destroy all infected leaves, including those on the ground. Do not water plants from above; wet leaves are hospitable to germinating spores.
Leaves, especially new leaves, become twisted or curled and are covered with a white powder. Flower buds and canes may also be affected.	Powdery mildew, a fungus disease carried by wind. The problem is most severe when nights are cool and humid, and days are warm and dry.	Remove and destroy all infected leaves, including those on the ground. To prevent mildew or to arrest its spread, apply a fungicide once every 10 days, starting in midspring.
Small red, brown or purple spots develop on upper leaf surfaces. The center of each spot eventually dries out, turns white and may fall out of the leaf. Leaves eventually turn yellow and fall from the plant.	Spot anthracnose, a fungus disease. The fungus spreads in water.	When symptoms appear, begin spraying with a fungicide once every seven days until all signs of the disease are eliminated. Do not water plants from above, since the fungus spreads in splashing water.
Rosebuds fail to open and are covered with a grayish brown, fuzzy mold. Open flowers are flecked with yellow or brown and lower petals are wilted and brown. The stems below infected flowers become discolored.	Botrytis blight, also called gray mold, a fungus disease that spreads in moist air and cool temperatures.	There are no chemical cures for blight once it occurs. If symptoms appear, cut off and destroy all infected plant parts. Spray with a fungicide to keep the disease from spreading.

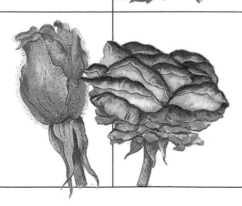

PROBLEM	CAUSE	SOLUTION
Red or brown sunken spots with dark margins develop on canes. Cracks may appear within the spots. The spots enlarge and eventually encircle the cane. Leaves and stems above the damaged area turn yellow, wilt and die.	Canker, a fungus disease. The fungus spreads in water and enters the plant through cuts or wounds in the canes. The problem is most severe in early to middle spring, when plants come out of dormancy.	There is no chemical preventive or cure for canker. When symptoms appear, prune infected canes below the canker. Use sharp pruning shears and make the cut just above a node at a 45° angle.
An orange, powdery substance appears on the undersides of the leaves. Eventually, yellow or brown spots appear on upper leaf surfaces. Infected leaves may wilt or curl.	Rust, a fungus disease that spreads in moist air and moderate temperatures. The problem is most severe in the Pacific Northwest, where the climate is cool and humid.	Remove and destroy all infected leaves, including those on the ground. Avoid overhead watering because the fungus spreads in water. To prevent the disease, spray with a fungicide every seven to 10 days in cool, wet weather.
Round growths about 2 inches in diameter appear at the base of the plant. The growths are light green when young and turn brown and woody as they age. Plant growth is stunted, foliage is abnormally small and few buds are produced.	Crown gall, a disease caused by bacteria that live in the soil. The bacteria enter a plant through the roots or through wounds at the root area. The bacteria cause abnormal cell growth, which produces the galls.	There are no chemical controls for crown gall. Small galls may be pruned out with a sharp knife or pruning shears. Disinfect tools with alcohol or household bleach after each cut. In severe cases, remove the plant and the soil surrounding the roots to prevent the bacteria from spreading.
Leaves are mottled or streaked with yellow *(A)* or they develop a pattern of yellow netting *(B)*. Plant growth slows.	Mosaic, a virus disease that is often transmitted by aphids and other insects. Although the virus does not affect flowers, it detracts from the overall appearance of the plant.	There are no chemical controls or cures. In mild cases, symptoms often disappear by themselves. In severe cases, infected plants should be removed to prevent the virus from spreading.

PROBLEM	CAUSE	SOLUTION
Holes appear in flowers and then in leaves. Light-colored flowers are especially susceptible.	Japanese beetles, shiny copper-and-green, hard-shelled insects up to ½ inch long. Beetles move from flower to flower, consuming the petals before they eat the leaves. They seem to be attracted to light-colored blossoms.	Pick beetles off plants by hand and destroy them. Spray the plants with an insecticide. In late summer and in spring, treat the ground around affected roses with a grub-controlling insecticide or with milky spore. In the fall, rake up fallen leaves; adult beetles spend the winter in plant debris.
Small, rounded holes appear in leaves. Eventually, the entire leaf surface between the veins disappears.	Rose slugs, the larvae of sawfly wasps. The slug is light green with a dark brown head and up to ½ inch long. Some species have shiny bodies; others are covered with hair. Rose slugs generally feed on the undersides of leaves; they do not eat buds and flowers.	Spray with an insecticide and make sure the insecticide covers the undersides of leaves.
Roses fail to blossom or existing buds suddenly turn black and die. The foliage and the stem surrounding affected buds may also blacken and die.	Rose midge, a fly larva that is white and 1/12 inch long. The larvae feed in clusters at the bases of rosebuds.	Prune off and destroy all infested plant parts. Spray plants with an insecticide and apply a systemic insecticide to the ground around the plants where the larvae pupate.
Buds do not open, or flowers are deformed. Petals have brownish yellow streaks and small dark spots or bumps. White and pastel roses are particularly susceptible.	Thrips, tiny orange insects with elongated bodies. Thrips feed at the bases of rosebuds and on the petals of open flowers. They seem to be attracted to light-colored blossoms.	To discourage thrips from attacking, spray plants with a systemic insecticide just before the buds open. If signs of thrip damage appear, remove and destroy infected flowers and buds. Spray infected plants with an insecticide. If the infestation is severe, repeat applications may be necessary.
Leaves curl, rosebuds and foliage wither or become distorted in shape. A clear, sticky substance that attracts ants appears on foliage.	Aphids, semitransparent insects ⅛ inch long that cluster on new growth and flower buds. They suck the juice from the plant and secrete the sticky substance. Aphids can carry and spread diseases.	Aphids may be knocked off plants with a stream of water. In severe infestations, spray with an insecticide or an insecticidal soap.
Plant growth slows. Leaves and flowers are smaller than normal. Leaves may turn yellow, wilt and drop. The roots are discolored and have small, knotty growths at their tips.	Nematodes, microscopic worms that dwell in the soil and feed on plant roots. A soil analysis is needed to confirm the presence of nematodes.	Remove infested plants and the surrounding soil. Do not plant roses in the same area for three years. If the problem persists, professional soil treatment may be needed.

PROBLEM	CAUSE	SOLUTION
Small circles or ovals appear in leaf margins.	Leafcutter bees, which are shiny black, blue or purple bees. The bees do not eat the foliage; they use leaf material to build their nests.	Prune out canes that have damaged foliage. Since leafcutter bees are pollinators of several crops, the use of chemicals to destroy the bees is not recommended.
Round or oval masses appear on stems and canes. Foliage wilts, turns yellow and drops from the plant. Growth is stunted and flowers are not produced.	Rose scales, ⅛-inch, white, gray or brown insects with crusty shells. Scales usually appear in clusters.	Prune out and destroy heavily infested canes. Spray plants with an insecticide. To prevent scale infestation, spray plants with horticultural oil in early spring.
Upper surfaces of leaves are covered with small yellow specks. Leaves may curl.	Leafhoppers, which are triangular, white or light yellow insects ⅛ to ⅝ inch long. They feed on the undersides of leaves and suck the sap from the foliage. Leafhoppers can carry and spread diseases.	Spray with an insecticide or insecticidal soap. In the fall, rake up leaves and remove weeds that can harbor leafhopper eggs through the winter.
Holes appear in unopened rosebuds. Leaves and stems may also have holes or may be chewed off.	Caterpillars, the larvae of moths and butterflies. Most are yellow or green and up to 1 inch long. Some, such as budworms, attack only the flowers; others eat the leaves and stems.	Spray with *Bacillus thuringiensis,* called Bt, a bacterium fatal to caterpillars but harmless to plants and other animals. If caterpillars return to your garden every spring, Bt can be sprayed in anticipation of the problem.
Leaves become dry and have a dull bronze sheen. Tiny specks may be visible on the undersides of the leaves. Eventually, thin webbing appears on the foliage.	Spider mites, nearly microscopic pests that may be red, black, yellow or green. To confirm their presence, shake a leaf over a piece of white paper; the mites will be visible moving against the white background. Mites proliferate in hot, dry weather.	Knock adults off plants with a strong stream of water. Spray with a miticide three times, three days apart. Use different miticides; mites may build up resistance to a single miticide. Mites produce new generations in a few days, so repeat treatments will be necessary.
Growing tips, foliage and canes wilt. Swollen areas up to 1 inch long appear on canes.	Borers, moth larvae that are white or yellow worms up to 1 inch long. Borers enter the canes through wounds and through pruned stem tips.	Cut off the affected area. Make the cut below the swelling on the cane to be sure you remove the borer. To prevent borers from entering canes, apply shellac or white glue to the exposed tips after pruning.

97

TIPS AND TECHNIQUES

A CARPET OF ROSES

If your yard has a steep slope that makes lawn mowing difficult, you can use certain roses as ground cover. Not only will they fill the area with colorful blossoms; they also help hold soil in place, reducing erosion. And roses grown as ground covers require little maintenance. They need only an occasional pruning to remove old woody canes.

The roses that can be grown as ground covers are low-growing and have trailing canes, such as *Rosa rugosa alba,* 'Sea Foam' and 'The Fairy'. You can encourage the formation of a strong, dense carpet if you make slight cuts in the bottoms of the canes with a sharp knife, and then secure the cut portions to the ground with a light covering of soil. Where they are in contact with the ground, the canes will soon sprout additional roots and, eventually, more top growth.

A JUMP START FOR BARE-ROOT ROSES

Newly planted bare-root roses can be slow to start growing. If your bare-root plants don't show signs of growth within two to four weeks, you can help them along so that they are established before the summer heat sets in.

The best way to encourage growth is to increase the humidity around the canes. You can mound up pre-moistened peat moss around the canes, and keep the peat moss moist until foliage appears. When the foliage is about 1 inch long, remove or wash away the peat moss. Or you can place a clear plastic bag over the canes, make several holes in the bag for ventilation and let the bag remain on the canes until growth appears.

CONTAINERS FOR ROSES

When you plant roses in containers *(pages 20-21),* you need to keep the roses supplied with water. Even large containers provide only limited space for soil and roots, so the plants may dry out quickly, especially in summer heat. This is particularly true of containers made of wood or clay, because both materials draw water from the soil at the expense of the plant.

You can retain moisture in such containers in either of two ways. One is to line the container with plastic before planting. Then poke a few drainage holes in the bottom of the plastic. The plastic also makes wood less susceptible to rot, since it keeps moisture away from the wood.

The other method is to plant roses in one container that can be placed within a larger container. Fill the space between the two containers with peat moss and keep it well watered. Some of the water passes from the peat moss through the wood or clay of the inner pot to the planting medium; at the same time, the peat moss insulates against summer heat.

BLOSSOMS THROUGHOUT THE GROWING SEASON

When roses are dormant, as most of them are from fall through winter and spring, the rose garden can be a barren scene. But a rose garden interspersed with other types of plants can be colorful from early spring to late fall.

In early spring, when rose plants are merely bare canes, bulbs such as crocus, daffodil, hyacinth and squill will blossom until the roses begin to develop leaves. Plant them between rosebushes and along the border of the rose bed.

For early summer, when the bulbs die back, plant perennials such as forget-me-not, basket-of-gold and candytuft, or annuals such as petunia, salvia and sweet alyssum; they will add different colors, shapes and textures to your garden before your roses bloom. For fall color, plant late-blooming bulbs such as agapanthus, autumn crocus and autumn daffodil.

ROSE HIPS

After the last roses of the season fade, the spent flowers that remain on the plants will produce hips, which are seedpods. Most rose hips turn bright orange or red, and give color to the garden as winter approaches.

In addition to their beauty, rose hips also have practical value. They are a natural food source. When left on the plants, they will attract birds to your yard, since birds like to feed on the seeds they contain. Or you can collect the rose hips for your own use. Hips are rich in vitamin C; research indicates they contain more C than citrus. They have a sweet taste and may be eaten raw; you need only cut them open, remove the seeds and rinse them. They may also be cooked and used in making teas, jams and jellies.

You should not eat rose hips from plants that have been treated with chemicals to control insects and diseases; some of these chemicals leave residues that cannot be washed off and are hazardous to health.

THE PHOTOGENIC ROSE

When your conscientious work in the garden pays off with a crop of spectacular roses, keep a record of your showy blossoms on film. Photographs will let you enjoy them for years after the flowers have faded.

For the best effects, use a single lens reflex (SLR) camera, which allows you to use different lenses, from telephotos for close-ups of single blossoms to wide-angle lenses that can frame an entire section of the garden. The SLR, with its settings for shutter speed and aperture, also gives you some control over light, focus and depth of field.

Light is a key to taking good photographs. Some photographers like to shoot on overcast days, because the light is bright and even; the harsh spots of sunlight present on a clear day can wash out bright colors. For moody, romantic shots, the best times of day are early morning, when the light is soft and roses glisten with dew, and evening, when the setting sun suffuses light with warm red tones.

Whatever the time of day, make sure there is little or no wind, since a breeze moving through the flowers can cause the photograph to be blurred.

To show your rose and its details to best advantage, move in close to the flower so it will fill the picture. A close-up eliminates distracting detail. To capture the rose in its most natural pose, bend down to rose level, rather than standing straight and shooting down at the top of the flower. Hold the camera just slightly above the rose and at an angle to it to capture its full form.

6
DICTIONARY OF ROSES

oses have evolved over millions and millions of years. Botanically they belong to a single genus, but thousands of varieties exist, and horticulturists designate them by classes. Some grow in the wild; these belong to a class called species roses. The remaining classes consist of cultivars that plant breeders have developed by crossing species roses with one another, species roses with hybrids and hybrids with other hybrids. The cultivated rose classes are further divided into "old garden roses" and "modern roses," depending on whether they were developed before or after 1867—the year that a French botanist crossed a hybrid perpetual with a tea rose and bred the first Western rose to bloom repeatedly, abundantly and reliably from spring to fall. That event launched the era of modern roses—and a plethora of new classes. Class is determined by descent from a common ancestor and by dominant physical characteristics. Today more than a dozen and a half classes are recognized by international rose societies.

The roses in the dictionary that follows are listed alphabetically by individual rose names. Each entry indicates the class to which the rose belongs, and describes its type of blossom. Wherever possible the date of introduction is given, indicating whether the rose is a new variety or an old one. This is useful in anticipating a rose's behavior, since older roses are often extremely winter-hardy; newer roses are likely to have been bred for such qualities as disease resistance. Other qualities that may be singled out where appropriate are fragrance, repeat bloom, and characteristics of leaf or flower. Flowers described as "button-eyed" or "quartered" will have, respectively, tight centers of unopened petals, or a ring of subsidiary whorls of petals around the center, almost like blooms within blooms.

Finally, the entries indicate each rose's tolerance to cold. Those labeled tender will need protection where temperatures dip below 10° F; semihardy roses, below 0° F; hardy roses, below −10° F; and extremely hardy roses, below −20° F. But it is well to remember that roses can be damaged as much by winter sun and wind as by dropping temperatures.

'ALBA SEMI-PLENA'

'ALFRED DE DALMAS'

'ALTISSIMO'

'Alba Semi-Plena'
Introduced 16th century or earlier

Class. Alba

Flowers. Semidouble, 2½ inches, soft white. Short buds quickly open to cupped flowers displaying prominent gold stamens. Flowers borne in clusters of six to eight. Pure, sweet fragrance. This was the White Rose of the House of York during the Wars of the Roses.

Bloom. Midseason; does not repeat.

Plant. Sturdy and arching, 6 to 8 feet, with gray-green, matte foliage. A large crop of long, orange-red fruit ripens in late summer or fall. The plant will support itself in a vase-shaped form, rather bare at the base; or it may be trained against a wall, fence or trellis. Alba roses will grow and bloom well in more shade than most roses. They are immune to the common rose fungus diseases. Extremely hardy.

Landscape and other uses. In borders, on walls, fences, trellises, and as a specimen shrub. 'Alba Semi-Plena' has only one season of bloom, but the disease-free gray-green foliage makes it a good garden shrub all season, and the orange-red fruits add a late show.

'Alfred de Dalmas', sometimes designated 'Mousseline'
Introduced 1855

Class. Moss

Flowers. Double, 2½ to 3 inches, blush pink, fading almost to white in sun. Flowers are cupped and when fully open show stamens that are yellow at first and later develop light brown tips. Sepals and upper stems are lightly coated with a brown, prickly moss. Flowers are borne in small clusters.

Bloom. Midseason; repeats very well, unlike other garden roses, if carefully maintained.

Plant. Upright and bushy, 3 feet, with bristly canes and matte, light green leaves borne very close to the flowers. Extremely hardy. A tough plant, but needs spring pruning (shorten canes by half or two-thirds), generous feeding and watering to give repeating bloom.

Landscape and other uses. In beds, borders and large containers. 'Alfred de Dalmas' combines well with other plants.

'Altissimo'
Introduced 1966

Class. Large-flowered climber

Flowers. Single, having seven petals, 4 to 5 inches. Blossoms are velvety blood red, cupped to flat. Stamens are yellow and show up brightly against the red; they darken slightly with age. Flowers are borne in small clusters and sometimes singly. Little scent.

Bloom. Midseason; repeats all season.

Plant. Tall, 6 to 8 feet, with large, matte, dark green leaves; young shoots are purplish red. Hips are large. Semihardy. Training the canes to grow horizontally will increase blossoming.

Landscape and other uses. On pillars, walls and fences, and as a freestanding shrub.

—

'America'
Introduced 1976

Class. Large-flowered climber

Flowers. Double, 4 to 5 inches, rich, unfading coral pink. Very full, high-centered form, opening from spiraled, pointed-ovoid buds. Flowers are generally borne in clusters, sometimes singly, and last well. Strong fragrance.

Bloom. Midseason; repeats fairly well.

Plant. Upright and bushy, 9 to 12 feet, with dark, semiglossy foliage. Unlike most other large-flowered climbers, 'America' produces flowers on new shoots as well as on older ones. Semihardy.

Landscape and other uses. On pillars, fences and walls, and as long-lasting cut flowers.

—

'Angel Face'
Introduced 1968

Class. Floribunda

Flowers. Double, 3 to 4 inches, deep mauve with ruffled petal edges toned ruby. Flowers are flat to cupped, showing yellow stamens and long-lasting. Blossoms are borne in small clusters and singly. Strong old-rose fragrance with slight spiciness.

Bloom. Midseason; repeats well all season.

Plant. Bushy and compact, 2 to 3 feet, with leathery, glossy, dark green leaves. In some areas 'Angel Face' suffers from black spot and mildew, which weaken the plants and reduce their winter hardiness. Otherwise semihardy.

Landscape and other uses. In beds, borders and low hedges, and as cut flowers and exhibition flowers.

—

'Apothecary's Rose', sometimes designated
Rosa gallica officianalis
Known in ancient times

Class. Gallica

Flowers. Semidouble, 3 to 3½ inches, flat-cupped. The color is pink to modern eyes, but historically this is the Red Rose of the House of Lancaster in the Wars of the Roses. Before the importation of the first China roses, about 1700, this was as red as European roses came. Yellow

'AMERICA'

'ANGEL FACE'

'APOTHECARY'S ROSE'

'ARCHDUKE CHARLES'

'BABY BETSY MCCALL'

'BABY DARLING'

stamens show brightly against the petals. Flowers are borne singly or in clusters of three or four; the flower stems are strong and erect. Quite fragrant. Gallica roses are spicier and less sweet than other old roses, and their fragrance intensifies as the flower dries. This characteristic, and medieval belief in the medicinal powers of scented roses, made the 'Apothecary's Rose' the basis of the perfume industry in Provins, France. It was cultivated there for conserves as early as the 14th century.

Bloom. Profuse at midseason and reasonably long-lasting in flower; does not repeat.

Plant. Upright and bushy, 3 to 4 feet. Canes are almost thornless, with a few small prickles and a general coating of harmless, tiny bristles. Leaves are matte, even rough, and medium green. The plant spreads freely by suckers if grown on its own roots. When bud-grafted onto an understock, the plant does not spread, but grows taller, to 4 or 4½ feet. Extremely hardy.

Landscape and other uses. In hedges, in beds with other plants and as specimens. Round red hips provide late-summer interest. Dried petals are good for potpourri.

'Archduke Charles'
Introduced 1840

Class. China

Flowers. Double, opening slowly to 3 inches. The final color of the slowly opening flower depends very much on the weather, and may be pale pink in prolonged cool, cloudy weather, or deep rose, sometimes crimson, in really hot sun. Fruity fragrance.

Bloom. Repeats well all season.

Plant. Bushy, 3 feet, with glossy leaves that are reddish when young. New canes, smooth with red thorns, spread out rather stiffly and evenly from the base: the plant is shaped like an ice-cream cone. Tender.

Landscape and other uses. In beds, borders and hedges, and in combination with other plants. The color changes of 'Archduke Charles' add interest to a garden.

'Baby Betsy McCall'
Introduced 1960

Class. Miniature

Flowers. Double, 1 inch, cupped, light pink with showy yellow stamens. Buds are spiraled in form. Flowers are borne singly and in small clusters. Fragrant.

Bloom. Midseason; repeats well all season.

Plant. Vigorous, bushy and compact, 8 to 12 inches. Semihardy and somewhat disease-resistant.

Landscape and other uses. In borders, edgings, beds and containers. 'Baby Betsy McCall' also grows well indoors.

'Baby Darling'
Introduced 1964

Class. Miniature

Flowers. Double, 1 to 1½ inches, blended of orange and salmon. Small, pointed bud. Flowers are borne singly and several together on short stems. They are long-lasting provided they are shaded from afternoon sun. Moderately fragrant.

Bloom. Midseason; repeats intermittently.

Plant. Bushy and spreading, 12 inches, with small, light green foliage. Tender.

Landscape and other uses. In borders, edgings, beds and containers.

'BAHIA'

'Bahia'
Introduced 1974

Class. Floribunda

Flowers. Double, 2½ to 3½ inches, cupped, orange blended with rose or salmon. Flowers occur singly and in large clusters. Slight, spicy fragrance.

Bloom. Midseason; repeats all season.

Plant. Upright, 3 feet, with dark green or bronzy, glossy foliage. Semihardy.

Landscape and other uses. In beds, borders and hedges, and as a tree rose.

'BEAUTY SECRET'

'Beauty Secret'
Introduced 1965

Class. Miniature

Flowers. Double, 1½ inches, medium red. Bud is long, pointed and spiraled, and opens to a high-centered form that holds well. Flowers are borne singly and in small clusters. Spent flowers drop their petals cleanly. Very fragrant.

Bloom. Heavy midseason; repeats very well.

Plant. Upright, bushy, 12 inches, with glossy green foliage. Semihardy.

Landscape and other uses. In borders, edgings and beds. 'Beauty Secret' grows well indoors. It is good for cutting and exhibition.

'BELLE DE CRECY'

'Belle de Crecy'
Introduced before 1829

Class. Gallica

Flowers. Very double, 2½ to 3½ inches, in many changing shades of pink and mauve splashed

105

'BETTY PRIOR'

'BEWITCHED'

with violet and lavender-gray. The petals are evenly arranged, and the open flower forms a flattened ball with short central petals folded over to a point that is known as a button eye. Flowers are borne in small clusters. Very strong fragrance.

Bloom. Midseason; does not repeat.

Plant. Upright, rounded and compact, 3½ to 4½ feet, with dark, gray-green, rough-textured leaves. Canes are slender and nearly thornless, but have many harmless bristles and are not stiff enough to hold up the weight of the flowers. They may be staked or allowed to sprawl. Extremely hardy.

Landscape and other uses. In beds and borders, and as cut flowers. Combines well with other plants. 'Belle de Crecy' provides valuable blending colors among other roses in the garden and in bouquets.

—

'Betty Prior'
Introduced 1935

Class. Floribunda

Flowers. Single, having five petals, 3 inches, cupped on opening and becoming flat saucers. Buds are carmine; flowers remain red in cool weather and turn medium pink in warm weather. Stamens are yellow and turn brown with age. Flowers are borne in clusters. Slight to moderately spicy fragrance.

Bloom. Early midseason; repeats steadily all season.

Plant. Bushy, vigorous and upright, 5 feet, with semiglossy, medium green leaves. Hardy.

Landscape and other uses. Its unusual height makes 'Betty Prior' good in hedges and as a specimen.

—

'Bewitched'
Introduced 1967

Class. Hybrid Tea

Flowers. Double, high-centered, 5 inches, medium rose pink and very even in color. Flowers are exceptionally long-lasting. Blooms are borne singly. Moderate to strong old-rose fragrance.

Bloom. Midseason; repeats all season.

Plant. Upright and willowy, 6 to 10 feet, with large, glossy, light to medium green foliage and green bark. Semihardy.

Landscape and other uses. In beds and borders, and as cut flowers.

'Blanc Double de Coubert'

Introduced 1892

Class. Shrub

Flowers. Double, 2½ to 3 inches, extraordinarily pure white with a distinctive papery texture. Narrow, scrolled buds open quickly. Flowers are borne in clusters. Strong, spicy, old-rose fragrance, apparent even at night.

Bloom. Early; repeats some all season.

Plant. A descendant of *R. rugosa,* with lush green, crinkled foliage that is typical of Rugosas. Upright and bushy, 4 to 6 feet. Canes are gray and extremely thorny. Hips are large and orange-red. 'Blanc Double de Coubert', like other Rugosa roses, grows well even in sandy soil and salt spray, and is a good rose for a seashore garden. Rugosa foliage is entirely immune to the common rose fungus diseases and resists most insect damage. But it seems allergic to some fungicides: spare your Rugosas when spraying other roses. Extremely hardy.

Landscape and other uses. As a specimen, in hedges and in combination with other plants. The distinctively crinkled, disease-free foliage is a great garden asset.

'BLANC DOUBLE DE COUBERT'

'Blossomtime'

Introduced 1951

Class. Large-flowered climber

Flowers. Double, 3½ to 4 inches, pink on the upper surfaces when fully opened, and deeper pink on the undersides. Buds are pointed and high-centered; petals fold back as they open. Flowers are borne in clusters of three to eight. Strong fragrance.

Bloom. Midseason; repeats some all season.

Plant. Upright and bushy, 6 to 8 feet, with light to medium green, semiglossy foliage. Semihardy.

Landscape and other uses. On pillars, trellises, fences and walls, as a sprawling shrub without supports and as cut flowers.

'BLOSSOMTIME'

'Blue Nile'

Introduced 1981

Class. Hybrid Tea

Flowers. Double, 4½ to 5 inches, mauve. To hold the color, plant in partial shade. Large buds are pointed and hold their form well. Flowers are borne singly or in clusters of two or three on stiff stems. Citrus fragrance.

Bloom. Midseason; repeats sparsely all season.

Plant. Upright and spreading, 3 feet, with olive green foliage. Semihardy.

Landscape and other uses. In beds and borders, and as cut flowers.

'BLUE NILE'

'BLUE RIBBON'

'BONICA'

'BRANDY'

'BROADWAY'

'Blue Ribbon'
Introduced 1984

Class. Hybrid Tea

Flowers. Double, 5 to 6 inches, silvery mauve. Bud is spiraled and opens quickly. Flowers are borne singly on short stems. Good, strong fragrance.

Bloom. Midseason; repeats all season, but is not a heavy bloomer.

Plant. Upright and bushy, 3 feet, with medium-sized glossy green leaves. Semihardy.

Landscape and other uses. In beds and borders, and as cut flowers.

'Bonica'
Introduced 1981

Class. Shrub

Flowers. Double, 2½ to 3½ inches, light pink. Buds are spiraled, deeper in color toward the center and open to cupped flowers with ruffled petals. Blossoms are borne in large, loose clusters. Little scent.

Bloom. Midseason; repeats well all season.

Plant. Spreading, 3 to 5 feet, with small, glossy, dark green leaves. Orange fruit develops in fall and persists through winter. Hardy and considerably disease-resistant; requires less spraying than most roses.

Landscape and other uses. In beds, borders and hedges.

'Brandy'
Introduced 1981

Class. Hybrid Tea

Flowers. Double, 4 to 4½ inches, apricot blended with yellow. Spiraled buds open quickly to loose blooms showing yellow stamens. Petals are yellow at the base, deeper apricot on the undersides. The colors fade in hot weather. Flowers are generally borne singly, but sometimes two or three to a cluster. Mild tea or fruit fragrance.

Bloom. Midseason; repeats all season.

Plant. Upright, 4 to 5 feet, with large, semiglossy green leaves. Semihardy.

Landscape and other uses. In beds and borders, and as cut flowers.

'Broadway'
Introduced 1985

Class. Hybrid Tea

Flowers. Double, 4 inches, rich yellow blended with pink. Form is high-centered; petal edges rolled back to dark pink points. Flowers are borne singly. Strong fragrance.

Bloom. Midseason; repeats all season.

Plant. Upright, 4 feet, with semiglossy dark green foliage. Semihardy.

Landscape and other uses. In beds and borders, and as cut flowers.

—

'Canadian White Star'
Introduced 1980

Class. Hybrid Tea

Flowers. Double, 5 inches, pure white. Long, pointed buds open to high-centered flowers. Petal edges fold back to form points, giving the open flowers a starry outline. Flowers are borne singly. Little scent.

Bloom. Midseason; repeats all season.

Plant. Upright, 4 feet, with glossy, dark green foliage. Semihardy.

Landscape and other uses. In beds and borders, and as cut flowers.

—

'Catherine Mermet'
Introduced 1869

Class. Tea

Flowers. Double, 3 inches, in varying shades. Inner petals are pale pink and salmon, and yellow at the base; outer petals are touched with rose pink or lilac. The petals have a translucent quality. Buds open to a high-centered form with petal edges folded back. Flowers are borne singly or in clusters of three or four on stems that arch gracefully. Spicy or fruity fragrance, strongest in cool weather.

Bloom. Midseason; repeats well all season; blooms well in hot weather.

Plant. Upright and arching, 4 feet, with glossy foliage that is coppery when young. Smooth wood with few thorns. Tender.

Landscape and other uses. In beds and borders, as a specimen and as cut flowers.

—

'Cecile Brunner', sometimes designated
'Sweetheart Rose'
Introduced 1881

Class. Polyantha; Climbing Polyantha

Flowers. Double, 1 to 1½ inches, pale pink with yellow at the base. Little spiraled buds that open to high-centered or rather loose flowers. Flowers are borne in loose clusters. The fragrance is tealike, light but definite.

Bloom. Late. The bush form repeats very steadily all season; the climbing form repeats intermittently after a heavy initial bloom.

'CANADIAN WHITE STAR'

'CATHERINE MERMET'

'CECILE BRUNNER'

'CENTURY TWO'

'CHARISMA'

'CHARLOTTE ARMSTRONG'

Plant. Shrub form is 3 to 4 feet; climbing form reaches 15 to 25 feet tall. The bush form has sparse, semiglossy dark green foliage. The climber has foliage so dense that it may sometimes hide some of the flowers. Both forms have rather smooth wood and few thorns. Tender.

Landscape and other uses. In beds, borders and arbors, on large trellises and walls, and climbing up tree trunks. Make excellent cut roses and boutonnieres.

'Century Two'
Introduced 1971

Class. Hybrid Tea

Flowers. Double, 4½ to 5 inches, medium pink with violet overtones. Long, pointed buds open to cupped flowers that are borne singly or in small clusters, with long-lasting quality. Moderate fragrance.

Bloom. Midseason; repeats all season.

Plant. Upright and bushy, 4 feet, with leathery green foliage. Semihardy.

Landscape and other uses. In beds and borders, and as cut flowers and exhibition flowers.

'Charisma'
Introduced 1977

Class. Floribunda

Flowers. Double, 2½ to 3 inches, scarlet with deep yellow at the petal bases. Flowers are borne singly or in clusters. Little fragrance.

Bloom. Midseason; repeats well.

Plant. Bushy, 3 feet, with maroon canes and dense, glossy, dark green foliage. Semihardy.

Landscape and other uses. In beds, borders and low hedges.

'Charlotte Armstrong'
Introduced 1940

Class. Hybrid Tea

Flowers. Double, 3 to 4 inches. Spiraled buds, almost red, open to loose blossoms that are bright, deep cherry pink. Flowers are borne singly on long stems. Light fragrance.

Bloom. Midseason; repeats all season.

Plant. Upright and compact, 4 to 5 feet, with dark, leathery foliage. Semihardy.

Landscape and other uses. In beds and borders, and as cut flowers.

'Cherish'

Introduced 1980

Class. Floribunda

Flowers. Double, 3 to 4 inches, pastel coral pink. Spiraled buds open to high-centered blossoms that are long-lasting. The flowers are borne singly and in clusters of 15 or 20. Light fragrance.

Bloom. Heavy in midseason; repeats all season.

Plant. Spreading, 3 feet, with large, dark green foliage. Semihardy.

Landscape and other uses. In beds, borders and low hedges, and as cut flowers and exhibition flowers.

'CHERISH'

'Chevy Chase'

Introduced 1939

Class. Rambler

Flowers. Very double, 1½ inches, crimson-red that holds well. The flowers are flat and packed with many intricately arranged short petals. No stamens show, but the flower may have a tiny chartreuse eye. Blossoms are borne in clusters of 10 to 20, and are long-lasting. Slight fragrance.

Bloom. Late; does not repeat.

Plant. Climber, 15 feet, with light green, wrinkled foliage. Unlike the large-flowered and hybrid tea climbers, this rambler needs to be pruned to the ground immediately after flowering. Strong new shoots quickly arise; they will produce the best of the next year's flowers. Exceptionally disease-resistant. Hardy.

Landscape and other uses. On tall pillars, arbors, pergolas, trellises, fences and walls.

'CHEVY CHASE'

'Chicago Peace'

Introduced 1962

Class. Hybrid Tea

Flowers. Very double, 5 to 5½ inches, with strong deep pink blended with yellow. Ovoid buds open to flowers that are deep, full and cupped. Flowers are usually borne singly. Slight fragrance.

Bloom. Midseason; repeats well all season.

Plant. Upright, 4½ to 5 feet, with stout canes and large, dark green, leathery leaves. Semihardy.

Landscape and other uses. In beds and borders, and as cut flowers.

'CHICAGO PEACE'

'CHRISTIAN DIOR'

'CHRYSLER IMPERIAL'

'CINDERELLA'

'Christian Dior'

Introduced 1958

Class. Hybrid Tea

Flowers. Very double, 4 to 4½ inches, vivid red. Spiraled buds open to high-centered, cupped flowers. Flowers borne singly. Slight fragrance.

Bloom. Midseason; repeats well all season.

Plant. Bushy, 4 to 5 feet, with glossy, leathery, dark green leaves. Susceptible to mildew. Petal edges may be damaged by hot sun. Best planted in a location that has afternoon shade. Semihardy.

Landscape and other uses. In beds and borders, and as cut flowers.

'Chrysler Imperial'

Introduced 1952

Class. Hybrid Tea

Flowers. Double, 4½ to 5 inches, rich crimson with darker shadings (later fading to magenta) and a velvety texture. Buds are spiraled and are borne singly. Heavy, old-rose fragrance.

Bloom. Midseason; repeats well all season.

Plant. Upright, 4 to 5 feet, with semiglossy, dark green leaves. Somewhat subject to mildew. Semihardy.

Landscape and other uses. In beds and borders, and as cut flowers.

'Cinderella'

Introduced 1953

Class. Miniature

Flowers. Very double, ¾ to 1 inch, white with touches of light pink. The petals are tightly and evenly arranged. Flowers are borne singly and in clusters. Spicy and tealike fragrance.

Bloom. Abundant in midseason; repeats well all season.

Plant. Upright, vigorous and compact, 10 inches, almost thornless, with semiglossy green leaves. Semihardy and easy to grow.

Landscape and other uses. In borders, edgings, beds and containers. Also grows well indoors.

'Circus'

Introduced 1956

Class. Floribunda

Flowers. Double, 3 inches, buff-yellow blending with with soft, rose red. Sunlight increases the red tones as the flower matures. Flowers are cupped and show yellow stamens. They are borne in large, loose clusters. Light, spicy fragrance.

Bloom. Midseason; repeats well.

Plant. Bushy, 2½ feet, with maroon canes and dense, semiglossy, dark green foliage. Semihardy.

Landscape and other uses. In beds, borders and low hedges.

'CIRCUS'

'Color Magic'
Introduced 1978

Class. Hybrid Tea

Flowers. Double, 5 inches, ivory to deep rose. Long, spiraled buds open to flat-cupped blossoms that show amber stamens. Flowers are borne mostly singly. Slight fragrance.

Bloom. Midseason; repeats all season.

Plant. Upright and well-branched, 3½ to 4 feet, with large, glossy dark green foliage. Semihardy.

Landscape and other uses. In beds and borders, and as cut flowers and exhibition flowers.

'COLOR MAGIC'

'Command Performance'
Introduced 1970

Class. Hybrid Tea

Flowers. Double, 3 to 4 inches, orange-red, the backs of the petals being slightly lighter in color. Long buds open to high-centered, loosely formed, long-lasting blossoms; petal edges roll back to points. Flowers are borne singly or in clusters. Strong fragrance.

Bloom. Midseason; repeats all season.

Plant. Upright, 3½ to 4½ feet, with medium to dark green leaves of heavy texture. Susceptible to mildew and may flower poorly in hot, humid weather. Semihardy.

Landscape and other uses. In beds and borders, and as cut flowers.

'COMMAND PERFORMANCE'

'Cornelia'
Introduced 1925

Class. Shrub

Flowers. Double, 1 to 1½ inches, coppery coral or apricot to strawberry pink. Tight buds open quickly to rosette blossoms showing yellow stamens. Colors are softer in the heat of summer, more vivid in cool autumn weather. Flowers are borne in small to very large (18-inch) clusters. Strong fragrance of spiced honey and fruit.

Bloom. Late midseason; repeats well all season, sometimes giving its best display in autumn.

Plant. A descendant of musk roses. Arching, 6 to 8 feet, with brown canes and bronzy foliage. Grows and blooms well in partial shade. Semihardy.

'CORNELIA'

'CRIMSON GLORY'

'CUPCAKE'

'DOLLY PARTON'

Landscape and other uses. As a specimen, in borders and in combination with other plants. May be trained to grow on walls, trellises and fences.

—

'Crimson Glory'
Introduced 1935

Class. Hybrid Tea

Flowers. Double, 3½ to 4½ inches, deep crimson, becoming purplish with age. Spiraled buds open to sightly cupped flowers. Petals have velvety texture and dark highlights. Flowers are borne singly and nod on slender stems. Rich old-rose fragrance.

Bloom. Midseason; repeats well all season.

Plant. Spreading, 2½ to 3½ feet, with reddish brown wood and leathery, dark green foliage. Semihardy. There is a climbing form, 'Climbing Crimson Glory', which is more vigorous and blooms very freely, but does not repeat as well as the original bush.

Landscape and other uses. In beds and borders, and as cut flowers.

—

'Cupcake'
Introduced 1981

Class. Miniature

Flowers. Very double, 1½ inches, clear, medium pink that holds well. Buds open to high-centered, long-lasting flowers. Flowers are borne singly and in clusters of two to five. No fragrance.

Bloom. Heavy in midseason; repeats well all season.

Plant. Bushy, 12 to 14 inches, with semiglossy green foliage. Semihardy.

Landscape and other uses. In borders, edgings and containers, and as cut flowers and exhibition flowers.

—

'Dolly Parton'
Introduced 1983

Class. Hybrid Tea

Flowers. Double, 5 to 6 inches, bright, dark orange-red. The color deepens in hot sun, so the center may be lighter than the outer petals. Flowers are high-centered, long-lasting and borne singly on strong stems. Intense and penetrating fragrance.

Bloom. Midseason; repeats well all season.

Plant. Upright, 5 to 6 feet tall, with glossy, dark green foliage. Young leaves are dark red. Semihardy.

Landscape and other uses. In beds and borders, and as cut flowers and exhibition flowers.

'Don Juan'
Introduced 1958

Class. Large-flowered climber

Flowers. Double, 4 to 5 inches, dark, velvety red, sometimes brushed with nearly black markings. Oval buds open slowly to long-lasting, high-centered or cupped blossoms. Flowers are borne singly and in small clusters. Strong fragrance.

Bloom. Midseason; repeats all season.

Plant. Upright, 8 to 10 feet, with glossy, dark green foliage. Semihardy.

Landscape and other uses. On pillars, trellises, fences and walls, and as cut flowers.

'Double Delight'
Introduced 1977

Class. Hybrid Tea

Flowers. Double, 5½ inches, cherry red surrounding a creamy white center. Buds open to high-centered blossoms. Flowers are borne singly. Strong, spicy fragrance.

Bloom. Midseason; repeats all season.

Plant. Bushy, 4 feet, with matte green foliage. Semihardy.

Landscape and other uses. In beds and borders, and as cut flowers and exhibition flowers.

'Dr. Huey'
Introduced 1920

Class. Large-flowered climber

Flowers. Semidouble, 2½ to 3½ inches, red developing into maroon and crimson tones. Spiraled buds quickly open to long-lasting, cupped flowers with light yellow stamens. Flowers are borne in small clusters. Slight scent.

Bloom. Midseason for weeks; does not repeat.

Plant. Arching, 12 to 15 feet, with semiglossy, dark green foliage. Hardy.

Landscape and other uses. On pillars, trellises, fences and walls. 'Dr. Huey' is often used as an understock.

'Duet'
Introduced 1960

Class. Hybrid Tea

Flowers. Double, 4 inches, in two shades of pink, the tops of the petals being light and the undersides dark. Buds are urn-shaped and open

'DON JUAN'

'DOUBLE DELIGHT'

'DR. HUEY'

'DUET'

'ESCAPADE'

'EUROPEANA'

'EVENING STAR'

to loose blossoms displaying the two colors. Nonfading. Flowers are borne mostly in clusters. Slight fragrance.

Bloom. Midseason; repeats very well all season.

Plant. Upright, vigorous and bushy, 4 to 5½ feet, with glossy green leaves.

Landscape and other uses. In beds, borders and hedges, and as cut flowers.

'Escapade'
Introduced 1967

Class. Floribunda

Flowers. Semidouble, 3 inches, rosy violet blending to white at the center, with long, dark amber stamens showing prominently against the white. Flowers are saucer-shaped and have about 12 petals. They are borne in clusters.

Bloom. Midseason; repeats consistently all season.

Plant. Upright and bushy, 2½ to 3 feet, with glossy, light green leaves. Semihardy.

Landscape and other uses. In beds, borders and low hedges, and as cut flowers.

'Esmeralda' see 'Keepsake'

'Europeana'
Introduced 1963

Class. Floribunda

Flowers. Double, ruffled, 3 inches, deep crimson. Blossoms are neat, full, cupped and long-lasting. Flowers are borne in large clusters. Little fragrance.

Bloom. Midseason; repeats strongly all season.

Plant. Bushy and spreading, 2 to 3 feet. Foliage is dark red when young and matures to a glossy dark green with reddish tints. Large flower clusters are sometimes top-heavy; planting in groups lets the stems support each other. Semihardy.

Landscape and other uses. In beds, borders and low hedges, and as cut flowers.

'Evening Star'
Introduced 1974

Class. Floribunda

Flowers. Double, 4 to 4½ inches, pure white with light yellow bases. Buds are pointed and open to spiraled, high-centered blossoms. Flowers are borne singly and in clusters. Slight fragrance.

Bloom. Midseason; repeats all season.

Plant. Upright and bushy, 3 to 3½ feet, with dark, bluish green leaves. Tender.

Landscape and other uses. In beds, borders and low hedges, and as cut flowers and exhibition flowers.

'FASHION'

'Fashion'
Introduced 1949

Class. Floribunda

Flowers. Double, 3 to 3½ inches, unfading, luminous coral-peach. Oval, spiraled buds open to cupped flowers showing yellow stamens. Flowers are borne singly and in small clusters. Slight fragrance.

Bloom. Midseason; repeats well all season.

Plant. Upright and bushy, 4 feet, with semiglossy, bronze-green leaves. Semihardy.

Landscape and other uses. In beds, borders and low hedges, and as cut flowers.

'FIRST EDITION'

'First Edition'
Introduced 1976

Class. Floribunda

Flowers. Double, 2 to 2½ inches. Buds are coral-orange and pointed, and open to coral-rose cupped flowers that usually show yellow anthers. The color is richest in cool weather. Flowers are borne mostly in large, flat-topped clusters. Slight fragrance.

Bloom. Midseason; repeats all season.

Plant. Upright, 3½ feet, with glossy, light green foliage. Semihardy.

Landscape and other uses. In beds, borders and low hedges, and as cut flowers and exhibition flowers.

'FIRST PRIZE'

'First Prize'
Introduced 1970

Class. Hybrid Tea

Flowers. Double, 5 to 6 inches, pink with ivory centers. Long, pointed buds open to high-centered flowers. Blossoms are borne singly or in small clusters. Moderate fragrance.

Bloom. Midseason; repeats all season.

Plant. Upright and spreading, 5 feet, with leathery, dark green foliage. Susceptible to fungus diseases. Tender.

Landscape and other uses. In beds and borders, and as cut flowers and exhibition flowers.

'FOLKLORE'

'Folklore'
Introduced 1977

Class. Hybrid Tea

Flowers. Double, 4½ inches, blending tones of orange. Long, pointed buds open gradually to high-centered, long-lasting blossoms. Flowers are borne singly or in clusters. Strong fragrance.

Bloom. Midseason; repeats all season, slowly but in strong flushes.

Plant. Upright and bushy, 4 to 5 feet, with glossy, medium green leaves. New canes may have a spurt of growth in late summer. Semihardy.

Landscape and other uses. In beds and borders, and as cut flowers and exhibition flowers.

'FRAGRANT CLOUD'

'Fragrant Cloud'
Introduced 1963

Class. Hybrid Tea

Flowers. Double, 5 inches, varying shades of orange-red. Color fades in hot sun. Flowers are high-centered and borne in clusters of up to 10 blooms. The scent is among the strongest of all roses, blending the fragrances of tea and old rose.

Bloom. Midseason; repeats well all season.

Plant. Upright and vigorous, 4 to 5 feet tall, with large, glossy, dark green leaves. Easy to grow. Semihardy.

Landscape and other uses. In beds and borders, and as cut flowers.

'FRENCH LACE'

'French Lace'
Introduced 1980

Class. Floribunda

Flowers. Double, 3 to 4 inches, white with tones of apricot at the center. Pointed buds open evenly to flat, long-lasting blossoms. Flowers are borne from one to 12 on a stem. Slight tea fragrance.

Bloom. Midseason; repeats all season.

Plant. Upright and bushy, 3½ feet, with small, semiglossy, dark green foliage. Semihardy.

Landscape and other uses. In beds, borders and low hedges, and as cut flowers and exhibition flowers.

'GENE BOERNER'

'Gene Boerner'
Introduced 1968

Class. Floribunda

Flowers. Double, 2½ to 3½ inches, pink. Pointed buds open to high-centered blossoms; petal edges turn back to form points. Flowers are borne singly or in clusters. Slight fragrance.

Bloom. Midseason; repeats all season.

Plant. Upright, 3½ to 5 feet, with glossy green foliage. Semihardy.

Landscape and other uses. In beds, borders and hedges, and as cut flowers and exhibition flowers.

'Ginger'
Introduced 1962

Class. Floribunda

Flowers. Double, 3 to 4 inches, orange-scarlet. Oval buds open to cupped blossoms. Flowers are borne in clusters on strong stems. Slight fragrance.

Bloom. Midseason; repeats all season.

Plant. Upright, bushy and compact, 3 feet, with glossy, dark green foliage. Semihardy.

Landscape and other uses. In beds, borders and low hedges, and as cut flowers.

'Gingersnap'
Introduced 1978

Class. Floribunda

Flowers. Double, 4 inches, deep, tangerine-colored. Urn-shaped buds open to ruffled, long-lasting blossoms. Flowers are borne singly or in small clusters on long stems. Light fruity fragrance.

Bloom. Midseason; repeats sparsely.

Plant. Upright, 3 feet, with glossy, deep green foliage. Semihardy.

Landscape and other uses. In beds and borders, and as cut flowers.

'Gold Medal'
Introduced 1982

Class. Grandiflora

Flowers. Double, 3½ to 4 inches, deep yellow, sometimes flushed with orange-red. Long, pointed buds open to high-centered, long-lasting blossoms. Flowers are borne singly or in clusters. Slight tea fragrance.

Bloom. Midseason; repeats all season.

Plant. Upright and bushy, 4 to 5½ feet, with glossy, dark green foliage. Semihardy.

Landscape and other uses. In beds and borders, and as cut flowers and exhibition flowers.

'GINGER'

'GINGERSNAP'

'GOLD MEDAL'

'GOLDEN SHOWERS'

'Golden Showers'
Introduced 1956

Class. Large-flowered climber

Flowers. Double, 3½ to 4 inches, yellow. Pointed buds open quickly to flat flowers showing red-tipped stamens. In hot sun the open flowers fade to ivory; if grown in partial shade, flowers will be fewer, but will hold their yellow color. Blossoms are borne singly and in clusters on strong stems. Sweet lemon fragrance.

Bloom. Midseason; repeats well all season.

Plant. Upright, 8 to 10 feet, with glossy, dark green foliage. Somewhat disease-resistant, and semihardy. Flowers are well distributed over the whole plant, not only on the upper portions.

Landscape and other uses. On pillars, trellises, walls and fences, and as cut flowers.

'GOLDEN WINGS'

'Golden Wings'
Introduced 1956

Class. Shrub

Flowers. Single, generally having five petals but sometimes up to 10, 4 to 5 inches, clear pale yellow becoming ivory. Long, pointed buds open to saucer-shaped blossoms having dark amber stamens in the centers. Flowers are borne singly and in clusters. Light fragrance of clover and spice.

Bloom. Early; repeats continually all season.

Plant. Upright, branching and vigorous, 5 feet, with matte, light green leaves and moderately thorny canes. Hips are orange and showy. Hardy. Shortening canes by about a third at spring pruning encourages compactness.

Landscape and other uses. In borders and hedges and in combination with other plants, and as cut flowers.

'Granada'
Introduced 1963

Class. Hybrid Tea

Flowers. Double, 4 to 5 inches, yellow flushed with pink and red. Spiraled buds open to high-centered blossoms that flatten as they mature. Flowers are borne singly and in clusters. Strong spicy fragrance.

Bloom. Midseason; repeats very well all season.

Plant. Upright, 4½ to 5½ feet, with glossy, dark green foliage. The leaf edges are distinctively serrated. Susceptible to mildew. Tender.

Landscape and other uses. In beds and borders, and as cut flowers and exhibition flowers.

'GRANADA'

'Grandpa Dickens' see 'Irish Gold'

'Handel'

Introduced 1965

Class. Large-flowered climber

Flowers. Double, 3½ inches, creamy white edged with bright rose pink that deepens on exposure to hot sunshine. Spiraled buds open to blossoms that may be high-centered or cupped. Flowers are borne in clusters. Slight fragrance.

Bloom. Midseason; repeats all season.

Plant. Upright, 12 to 15 feet, with glossy, dark green foliage. Semihardy.

Landscape and other uses. On trellises, walls and fences.

'Hansa'

Introduced 1905

Class. Shrub

Flowers. Double, 3 to 3½ inches, bright red-violet. Long, slender bud quickly opens to a loose, crumpled flower. Flowers are borne in clusters on short stems. Strong fragrance of clove and old rose.

Bloom. Early; repeats well all season.

Plant. A descendant of *R. rugosa,* with dark green, crinkled foliage typical of Rugosas. Upright and bushy, 4 to 5 feet. Canes are gray and extremely thorny. Hips are large, round and orange-red. Like other Rugosa roses, 'Hansa' grows well even in sandy soil and salt spray, and is a good rose for a seashore garden. Its foliage is immune to the common rose fungus diseases and resists most insect damage. But it seems allergic to some fungicides. Spare Rugosas when spraying other roses. Extremely hardy.

Landscape and other uses. In hedges, in combination with other plants and as specimens. The crinkled, disease-free foliage is an asset in the garden. Use 'Hansa' where the penetrating fragrance can be enjoyed—near a doorway, a window, a porch or a patio.

'Heidi'

Introduced 1978

Class. Miniature

Flowers. Double, 1½ inches, bright pink, with mossy sepals. Urn-shaped buds open to blossoms that may be high-centered to cupped. Flowers are borne singly and in clusters. Strong sweet fragrance.

Bloom. Midseason; repeats well.

Plant. Bushy and vigorous, 12 inches, with glossy, medium to dark green foliage. Semihardy.

Landscape and other uses. In borders, edgings and containers. Also grows well indoors.

'HANDEL'

'HANSA'

'HEIDI'

'HERITAGE'

'HONOR'

'ICEBERG'

'Heritage'
Introduced 1985

Class. Shrub

Flowers. Double, 3 inches, blush pink, a little deeper toward the centers. The outer petals open to a deep cup surrounding a profusion of inner petals. Flowers are borne singly and in clusters. Strong and unusual fragrance that is a blend of old rose, myrrh and lemon.

Bloom. Midseason; repeats all season.

Plant. Upright, 4 feet, with semiglossy, dark green foliage. May be pruned like a hybrid tea to produce a smaller plant with larger flowers. Semihardy.

Landscape and other uses. In beds, borders and in combination with other plants, and as cut flowers.

'Hidcote Yellow' see 'Lawrence Johnston'

'Honor'
Introduced 1980

Class. Hybrid Tea

Flowers. Double, 4 to 5 inches, white. Pointed buds open slowly to loose blossoms. Flowers are borne singly and in clusters. Light fragrance.

Bloom. Midseason; repeats all season.

Plant. Upright and bushy, 5 to 5½ feet, with large, dark green foliage. Tender.

Landscape and other uses. In beds and borders, and as cut flowers and exhibition flowers.

'Iceberg', sometimes designated 'Schneewittchen'
Introduced 1958

Class. Floribunda

Flowers. Double, 2½ to 3½ inches, pure white. Spiraled buds open to loosely cupped blossoms. Flowers are borne in small and large clusters. Mild, sweet fragrance.

Bloom. Abundant in early part of midseason; repeats well all season.

Plant. Upright and bushy, 3 to 4½ feet, with glossy, light green foliage and few thorns. Forms a rounded bush if given room to spread. Hardy.

Landscape and other uses. In beds, borders and hedges, and as cut flowers and exhibition flowers. Makes an excellent tree rose.

'Intrigue'
Introduced 1984

Class. Floribunda

Flowers. Double, 3 inches, rich plum purple. Spiraled buds open to high-centered blossoms. Flowers are borne singly or in small clusters. Strong fragrance of lemon and old rose.

Bloom. Midseason; repeats all season.

Plant. Upright and branching, 3 feet, with semiglossy, dark green foliage. Tender.

Landscape and other uses. In beds and borders, and as cut flowers.

—

'Irish Gold', sometimes designated 'Grandpa Dickens'
Introduced 1966

Class. Hybrid Tea

Flowers. Double, 6 to 7 inches, light yellow that may be slightly shaded with green or edged with pink. Blossoms are high-centered and long-lasting; petals fold back to form points. Flowers are generally borne singly. Hot weather reduces flower size and quality. Slightly sweet fragrance.

Bloom. Midseason; repeats all season.

Plant. Upright and bushy, 3 to 4½ feet, with glossy foliage. Susceptible to fungus diseases. Tender.

Landscape and other uses. In beds and borders, and as cut flowers.

—

'Ivory Fashion'
Introduced 1958

Class. Floribunda

Flowers. Semidouble, 3½ to 4½ inches, ivory white flowers. Oval buds open to wide, slightly cupped flowers showing dark amber and yellow stamens. Flowers are borne in clusters. Moderate fragrance.

Bloom. Midseason; repeats all season.

Plant. Upright and branching, 3 feet, with semiglossy, green foliage. Semihardy.

Landscape and other uses. In beds, borders and low hedges, and as cut flowers and exhibition flowers.

—

'Jean Kenneally'
Introduced 1984

Class. Miniature

Flowers. Double, 1½ inches, apricot blended with yellow and pink. Blossoms are spiraled, high-centered and long-lasting; petals fold back to form points. Flowers are borne singly and in clusters. Slight fragrance.

'INTRIGUE'

'IRISH GOLD'

'IVORY FASHION'

'JEAN KENNEALLY'

123

Bloom. Midseason; repeats very well all season.

Plant. Upright, bushy and vigorous, 22 to 30 inches (tall for a miniature). Semihardy.

Landscape and other uses. In borders, beds and containers, and as cut flowers and exhibition flowers.

'JOSEPH'S COAT'

'Joseph's Coat'
Introduced 1964

Class. Large-flowered climber

Flowers. Double, 3 inches, with changing tones of yellow, pink and red. Urn-shaped buds open to cupped blossoms. Flowers are borne in clusters. Slight fragrance.

Bloom. Midseason; repeats all season.

Plant. Upright, 8 to 10 feet, with glossy, dark green foliage. Unlike most climbers, 'Joseph's Coat' blooms on new wood. Tender.

Landscape and other uses. On pillars, trellises, walls and fences. Can be grown as a freestanding shrub of about 6 feet.

'KATHERINE LOKER'

'Katherine Loker'
Introduced 1978

Class. Floribunda

Flowers. Double, 3½ inches, bright yellow. Pointed buds open to cupped blossoms that are long-lasting. Flowers are borne singly in small clusters. Slightly spicy fragrance.

Bloom. Midseason; repeats well all season.

Plant. Upright and spreading, 2½ to 3 feet, with semiglossy foliage. Tender.

Landscape and other uses. In beds and borders, and as cut flowers.

'KEEPSAKE'

'Keepsake', sometimes designated 'Esmeralda'
Introduced 1981

Class. Hybrid Tea

Flowers. Double, 5 inches, blended light and dark pink. Oval buds open to high-centered blossoms. Flowers are borne singly or in clusters of two or three. Moderate fragrance.

Bloom. Midseason; repeats all season.

Plant. Upright and bushy, 5 to 6 feet, with glossy green foliage and large, heavy thorns. Semihardy.

Landscape and other uses. In beds and borders, and as cut flowers and exhibition flowers.

124

'Kentucky Derby'
Introduced 1972

Class. Hybrid Tea

Flowers. Double, 5 inches, clear, dark red that holds well even in hot weather. Pointed buds and high-centered blossoms that are long-lasting. Flowers are generally borne singly. Slight fragrance.

Bloom. Midseason; repeats all season.

Plant. Upright and bushy, 5 to 6 feet, with glossy green foliage. Semihardy.

Landscape and other uses. In beds and borders, and as cut flowers.

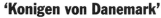

'KENTUCKY DERBY'

'Konigen von Danemark'
Introduced 1826

Class. Alba

Flowers. Very double, 2½ to 3½ inches, light pink shading to deeper pinks at the center. Short buds open to quartered form and a button eye. Flowers are borne singly or in small clusters. Intense, sweet fragrance.

Bloom. Midseason; does not repeat.

Plant. Upright and open, 5 to 6 feet, with matte, dark blue-green foliage. To keep plant compact prune canes to about 2 feet in spring. Immune to black spot and mildew. Extremely hardy.

Landscape and other uses. In beds and borders, in combination with other plants, on walls, fences, pillars and trellises, and as cut flowers.

'KONIGEN VON DANEMARK'

'Lady Hillingdon'
Introduced 1910

Class. Tea

Flowers. Semidouble, 3½ inches, apricot-yellow that fades in hot sun. Long, pointed, spiraled buds open to loosely formed blossoms. Flowers are borne singly and in clusters, nodding on slender stems.

Bloom. Early midseason; repeats well all season.

Plant. Upright and bushy, 2½ to 3½ feet, with canes and foliage that are purple or coppery when young and glossy, dark green when mature. Few thorns. Somewhat disease-resistant. Tender. A climbing form, 'Climbing Lady Hillingdon', grows to 15 feet in height.

Landscape and other uses. In beds and borders, and as cut flowers. 'Climbing Lady Hillingdon' may be used on trellises, arbors and walls.

'LADY HILLINGDON'

'LADY X'

'LAMARQUE'

'LANVIN'

'LA REINE VICTORIA'

'Lady X'
Introduced 1966

Class. Hybrid Tea

Flowers. Double, 4½ to 5 inches, pale mauve. Long, pointed buds open to high-centered blossoms. Flowers are generally borne singly on long stems. They are easily damaged by rain, and petal edges may burn in very hot weather. Slight fragrance.

Bloom. Midseason; repeats all season.

Plant. Upright and branching, 5 to 7 feet, with sparse, semiglossy foliage. Semihardy.

Landscape and other uses. In beds and borders, and as cut flowers.

'Lamarque'
Introduced 1830

Class. Noisette

Flowers. Double, 2 inches, pale yellow fading to white, with lemon yellow centers. Spiraled buds open to flat blossoms with rolled petals. Flowers are borne in loose clusters on nodding stems. Sweet, spicy tealike fragrance.

Bloom. Midseason; repeats sparsely.

Plant. Climbing and vigorous, 10 to 15 feet, with glossy, light green foliage. Tender.

Landscape and other uses. On walls, fences and arbors.

'Lanvin'
Introduced 1986

Class. Hybrid Tea

Flowers. Double, 3 to 4 inches, yellow. Pointed buds open to high-centered blossoms. Flowers are borne in clusters of three to five. No fragrance.

Bloom. Midseason; repeats all season.

Plant. Upright and bushy, 3 feet, with semiglossy, reddish green leaves. Semihardy.

Landscape and other uses. In beds and borders, and as cut flowers.

'La Reine Victoria'
Introduced 1872

Class. Bourbon

Flowers. Double, 2½ to 3½ inches, lilac-pink to deep rose; the color is pale in cool, cloudy weather and deepens in strong sun. Blossoms are cupped and long-lasting; petals are shell-shaped, overlapping and silky in texture. Flowers are borne singly and in clusters. Strong fragrance with a hint of fruit.

Bloom. Abundant in midseason; repeats throughout the season.

Plant. Slender and upright, 4½ to 6 feet, with soft, semimatte, green foliage and few thorns. The canes are slender; they need support or pegging down to produce a full display of flowers all along the canes. Hardy.

Landscape and other uses. In beds, borders and in combination with other plants, on pillars, as a specimen shrub and as cut flowers.

'Las Vegas'
Introduced 1981

Class. Hybrid Tea

Flowers. Double, 5 inches, orange-red blended with salmon and yellow tones. Long, pointed buds open quickly to blossoms that are high-centered at first and become loose as they mature. Flowers are borne one to three on a stem. Slight fragrance.

Bloom. Abundant in midseason; repeats throughout the season.

Plant. Upright and bushy plant, 4 feet, with leathery, semiglossy, green foliage. Semihardy.

Landscape and other uses. In beds and borders, and as cut flowers.

'Lavender Jewel'
Introduced 1978

Class. Miniature

Flowers. Double, 1 to 1½ inches, lavender-mauve, sometimes edged with magenta. Pointed buds open to full, high-centered blossoms. Flowers are generally borne in clusters of three to five, but sometimes singly. Slight fragrance.

Bloom. Midseason; repeats well all season.

Plant. Bushy and spreading, 10 inches tall and somewhat wider, with glossy, dark green leaves. Semihardy.

Landscape and other uses. In borders, edgings, beds and containers. Because of its spreading habit, 'Lavender Jewel' is a good plant for a hanging basket. It also makes good cut flowers and exhibition flowers.

'Lawrence Johnston', sometimes designated 'Hidcote Yellow'
Introduced after 1923

Class. Large-flowered climber

Flowers. Semidouble, 3 to 3½ inches, bright yellow. Blossoms are cupped and show prominent yellow stamens. Flowers are borne in clusters. Rich fragrance.

'LAS VEGAS'

'LAVENDER JEWEL'

'LAWRENCE JOHNSTON'

'LOVE'

'MADAME HARDY'

'MADAME ISAAC PEREIRE'

Bloom. Early to midseason; repeats sparsely and intermittently.

Plant. Upright, 20 feet, with glossy, light green leaves and thorny canes. Susceptible to black spot in warm climates. Hardy.

Landscape and other uses. On trellises, fences and walls. Can be grown as a freestanding shrub 6 to 10 feet tall.

'Love'
Introduced 1980

Class. Grandiflora

Flowers. Double, 3½ inches, sharply bi-colored, red and white. Spiraled buds open to high-centered blossoms. Petal edges roll back to form points, making the play of contrasting colors very effective in the bud and in the half-open bloom. Flowers are borne singly and in clusters. Little fragrance.

Bloom. Midseason; repeats very well all season.

Plant. Stiffly upright, 3 to 4 feet, with matte, dark green leaves and thorny canes. Semihardy.

Landscape and other uses. In beds and borders, and as cut flowers and exhibition flowers.

'Madame Hardy'
Introduced 1832

Class. Damask

Flowers. Very double, 3 to 3½ inches. Bud is flesh pink and opens to an ivory white blossom. The many petals are intricately folded in sections, with a green button eye at the center. Leafy sepals ornament the unopened buds. Flowers are borne in clusters. Soft, delicate fragrance.

Bloom. Abundant in midseason; does not repeat.

Plant. Upright, bushy and vigorous, 5 feet, with green leaves and thorny canes. Canes may droop under the weight of the flowers. To keep them upright, bind the canes together, stake them or situate several plants together for mutual support. Disease-resistant. Extremely hardy.

Landscape and other uses. In borders, in combination with other plants and as cut flowers.

'Madame Isaac Pereire'
Introduced 1881

Class. Bourbon

Flowers. Double, 4 to 5 inches, deep purplish pink. Blossoms are deep and quartered in form, with rolled petal edges. Flowers are borne in small clusters. Powerful fragrance with some fruitiness.

Bloom. Midseason; repeats moderately, but the largest flowers of best form may bloom in September.

Plant. Upright and bushy, 5 to 6 feet or taller; some canes will shoot up more than 6 feet in a season. Profits from pegging down. Leaves are large, semiglossy, dark green. 'Madame Isaac Pereire' is tough and will grow even in poor soil. Hardy.

Landscape and other uses. In borders, in combination with other plants, on pillars, as cut flowers and for potpourri. May be grown as a small climber.

'Maiden's Blush'
Introduced before 1500

Class. Alba

Flowers. Very double (as many as 200 petals), 3 inches, shades of pink to creamy white. Flowers are borne mostly in small clusters and are long-lasting. Pure, sweet fragrance.

Bloom. Abundant in early midseason; does not repeat.

Plant. Arching, bushy and vigorous, 8 feet, with blue-green foliage having a grayish coating. Unusually tolerant of shade and immune to the common fungus diseases. Extremely hardy.

Landscape and other uses. As a specimen, in hedges, in combination with other plants and as cut flowers. May be pegged down or trained against a wall.

'Marina'
Introduced 1974

Class. Floribunda

Flowers. Double, 2½ to 3 inches, deep, unfading orange, with yellow at the base. Long, pointed buds open to high-centered blossoms. Flowers are borne in clusters. Light fragrance.

Bloom. Midseason; repeats well all season.

Plant. Upright, 3 feet tall, with glossy, dark green foliage. Semihardy.

Landscape and other uses. In beds and borders, and as cut flowers.

'Mary Marshall'
Introduced 1970

Class. Miniature

Flowers. Double, 1½ inches, blended tones of orange, yellow and coral. Long, pointed buds open to cupped, long-lasting blossoms. Flowers are borne singly and in clusters. Moderate fragrance.

'MAIDEN'S BLUSH'

'MARINA'

'MARY MARSHALL'

129

'MARY ROSE'

'MATADOR'

'MEDALLION'

Bloom. Midseason; repeats well all season.

Plant. Upright and bushy, 10 to 14 inches, with semiglossy, green foliage. Semihardy.

Landscape and other uses. In borders, edgings, beds and containers, and as cut flowers and exhibition flowers. May be grown indoors, but is slow to repeat-bloom.

—

'Mary Rose'
Introduced l983

Class. Shrub

Flowers. Double, 3 to 4 inches, soft, rose pink that pales with age. Short buds open quickly to loosely cupped flowers having short petals. Flowers are borne in clusters. Sweet fragrance.

Bloom. Abundant in early midseason; repeats well all season.

Plant. Upright and arching, 4½ feet, with matte, light to medium green foliage. Pruned severely in the manner of a hybrid tea, 'Mary Rose' will make a smaller bush with larger flowers; pruned very lightly it makes a larger, looser shrub. Disease-resistant. Hardy.

Landscape and other uses. In beds, borders and in combination with other plants, and as a specimen.

—

'Matador'
Introduced 1972

Class. Floribunda

Flowers. Double, 2½ inches, scarlet and yellow. The upper petal surface is orange-scarlet, the underside yellow. Oval buds open to high-centered, long-lasting blossoms. Flowers are borne singly or in clusters. Little fragrance.

Bloom. Midseason; repeats all season.

Plant. Bushy and vigorous, 3 feet, with large, dark green, leathery leaves and many thorns.

Landscape and other uses. In beds and borders, and as cut flowers.

—

'Medallion'
Introduced 1973

Class. Hybrid Tea

Flowers. Double, 6 to 8 inches, light apricot. Long, pointed buds open quickly to loosely formed open blossoms. Flowers are borne singly. Moderate, fruity fragrance.

Bloom. Midseason; repeats all season.

Plant. Upright and slightly spreading, 5 to 6 feet, with large, green, leathery leaves. The weight of the large flowers may bend the canes over, especially after rain. Tender.

Landscape and other uses. In beds and borders, and as cut flowers.

'Minnie Pearl'
Introduced 1982

Class. Miniature

Flowers. Double, 1½ inches, light pink blended with apricot; petal bases are light yellow. Color deepens slightly in hot sun. Long, pointed buds open to high-centered blossoms. Flowers are borne singly. Slight fragrance.

Bloom. Midseason; repeats well all season.

Plant. Upright and branching, 18 to 24 inches, with semiglossy, green foliage. Semihardy.

Landscape and other uses. In borders, edgings, beds and containers, and as cut flowers and exhibition flowers.

'Mister Lincoln'
Introduced 1964

Class. Hybrid Tea

Flowers. Double, 5 to 6 inches, dark, unfading red with velvety petal texture. Pointed buds open to high-centered, long-lasting blooms that become cupped or globular. Flowers are borne singly on long, stiff stems. Strong, rich fragrance.

Bloom. Midseason; repeats all season, but sparsely.

Plant. Upright, branching and vigorous, 4½ to 5½ feet, with matte or semiglossy, dark green leaves. The foliage is less disease-prone than other dark red hybrid teas and the plant is easy to grow. Semihardy.

Landscape and other uses. In beds and borders, and as cut flowers and exhibition flowers.

'Mousseline' see 'Alfred de Dalmas'

'Mrs. John Laing'
Introduced 1887

Class. Hybrid Perpetual

Flowers. Double, 4 inches, soft, silvery pink. Short, pointed buds open to full, cupped blossoms, having inner petals a little shorter than the outer. Flowers borne singly and in small clusters. Strong fragrance.

Bloom. Midseason; repeats well all season.

Plant. Upright, 3 to 4 feet, with matte, light green leaves and few thorns. Hardy.

Landscape and other uses. In beds, borders and in combination with other plants, and as cut flowers.

'MINNIE PEARL'

'MISTER LINCOLN'

'MRS. JOHN LAING'

'NEW DAWN'

'New Dawn'
Introduced 1930

Class. Large-flowered climber

Flowers. Double, 3 inches, translucent, blush pink and a little darker toward the center. Spiraled buds open to cupped blossoms that show stamens. Flowers are generally borne in clusters but sometimes singly. Sweet tea fragrance.

Bloom. Late midseason; repeats well all season.

Plant. Upright, spreading and vigorous, 12 to 20 feet tall, with glossy, dark green leaves and thorny canes. Can be grown without support as a mounding shrub. Will grow well in partial shade, but produces fewer flowers than in the sun. Immune to the common fungus diseases. Hardy.

Landscape and other uses. On pillars, trellises, walls and fences, and as cut flowers. Can be trained to climb up a small tree trunk.

'OLDTIMER'

'Oldtimer'
Introduced 1969

Class. Hybrid Tea

Flowers. Double, 7 inches, pale apricot with a bronze cast. Long, pointed buds open quickly to high-centered, long-lasting blossoms. Flowers are borne singly. Slight fragrance.

Bloom. Midseason; repeats all season but not abundantly.

Plant. Upright and vigorous, 3 to 4 feet, with glossy green foliage. Semihardy.

Landscape and other uses. In beds and borders, and as cut flowers.

'OLYMPIAD'

'Olympiad'
Introduced 1984

Class. Hybrid Tea

Flowers. Double, 4 to 5 inches, bright, unfading red with velvety petal texture. Unlike most red roses, 'Olympiad' does not turn bluish with age. Pointed buds open to high-centered, long-lasting blossoms. Flowers are borne singly or in small clusters. Very slight fragrance.

Bloom. Abundant in midseason; repeats well all season.

Plant. Upright and bushy, 3 to 5 feet, with semiglossy green foliage and thorny canes. Semihardy.

Landscape and other uses. In beds and borders, and as cut flowers and exhibition flowers.

'Orangeade'
Introduced 1959

Class. Floribunda

Flowers. Semidouble, 2½ to 3½ inches, clear orange. Small buds open quickly to blossoms showing bright yellow stamens. Flowers are borne in clusters. Slight fragrance.

Bloom. Midseason; repeats all season.

Plant. Bushy and vigorous, 2½ to 3 feet, with round, dark green leaves. Susceptible to mildew. Semihardy.

Landscape and other uses. In beds and borders, and as cut flowers.

'ORANGEADE'

'Orange Sunblaze'
Introduced 1982

Class. Miniature

Flowers. Double, 1½ inches, bright, unfading orange-red. Short buds open to flat rosettes. No fragrance.

Bloom. Midseason; repeats well all season.

Plant. Upright and bushy, 12 to 16 inches, with large, matte, light green foliage. Semihardy.

Landscape and other uses. In beds, borders, edgings and containers.

'ORANGE SUNBLAZE'

'Oregold'
Introduced 1975

Class. Hybrid Tea

Flowers. Double, 4½ to 5 inches, deep, unfading yellow. Oval buds open to high-centered blossoms; petals roll back to form points. Flowers are borne on long stems, singly or in small clusters. Slight fragrance.

Bloom. Midseason; repeats sparsely.

Plant. Upright and branching, 3 to 4 feet, with large, glossy, dark green foliage and strong, moderately thorny canes. Tender.

Landscape and other uses. In beds and borders, and as cut flowers.

'OREGOLD'

'Pacesetter'
Introduced 1979

Class. Miniature

Flowers. Double, 1¾ inches, pure white. Long, pointed buds open to high-centered blossoms. Flowers are generally borne singly on long stems. Fragrant.

Bloom. Midseason; repeats all season.

Plant. Upright, 18 to 24 inches, with matte, dark green foliage. Semihardy.

'PACESETTER'

'PAPA MEILLAND'

'PARTY GIRL'

'PASCALI'

Landscape and other uses. In beds, borders, edgings and containers.

—

'Papa Meilland'
Introduced 1963

Class. Hybrid Tea

Flowers. Double, 5 to 6 inches, bright, dark crimson brushed with black on petals. Pointed buds open to high-centered blossoms. Flowers are borne singly. Strong fragrance.

Bloom. Midseason; repeats all season.

Plant. Upright, 4 to 5 feet, with large, dark green foliage. Occasionally one cane will grow much taller than the others; it may be pinched back as it grows or allowed to bloom and then pruned to restore the shape of the bush. Susceptible to fungus diseases. Semihardy.

Landscape and other uses. In beds and borders, and as cut flowers.

—

'Party Girl'
Introduced 1979

Class. Miniature

Flowers. Double, 1½ inches, soft yellow with tones of apricot-pink. Long, pointed buds open to high-centered blossoms. Flowers are usually borne singly, sometimes in large clusters. Spicy fragrance.

Bloom. Midseason; repeats all season.

Plant. Upright and bushy, 12 to 15 inches, with semiglossy, dark green foliage. Semihardy.

Landscape and other uses. In beds, borders, edgings and containers, and as cut flowers and exhibition flowers. Grows well indoors.

—

'Pascali'
Introduced 1963

Class. Hybrid Tea

Flowers. Double, 3 to 4 inches, creamy white, sometimes spotted with pink in wet weather. Pointed buds open to high-centered blossoms. Flowers are borne singly or in clusters. Little fragrance.

Bloom. Midseason; repeats well all season.

Plant. Upright, 3½ to 4 feet, with semiglossy, dark green leaves. Semihardy.

Landscape and other uses. In beds and borders, and as cut flowers and exhibition flowers.

'Peace'
Introduced 1945

Class. Hybrid Tea

Flowers. Double, 5 to 6 inches, light yellow edged with pink, except in cool weather, when the pink may be missing. Plump, spiraled buds open to high-centered blossoms. Flowers are borne singly or in clusters. Slight fragrance.

Bloom. Midseason; repeats well all season.

Plant. Upright and bushy, 4 to 5½ feet, with large, glossy, dark green foliage and thick, moderately thorny canes. Semihardy.

Landscape and other uses. In beds, borders and in combination with other plants, and as cut flowers and exhibition flowers.

'PEACE'

'Perfume Delight'
Introduced 1973

Class. Hybrid Tea

Flowers. Double, 4 to 5 inches, rose pink. Long, pointed buds open to cupped blossoms. Flowers are borne singly or in clusters. Strong, spicy fragrance.

Bloom. Midseason; repeats all season.

Plant. Upright and bushy, 3 to 4½ feet, with large green leaves and strong, thick, thorny canes. Semihardy.

Landscape and other uses. In beds and borders, and as cut flowers.

'PERFUME DELIGHT'

'Perle d'Or'
Introduced 1884

Class. Polyantha

Flowers. Very double, 2 inches, apricot that pales to buff. Spiraled buds open to flat blossoms having many narrow, often folded, petals at the center. Flowers are borne singly and in clusters. Slight fragrance.

Bloom. Midseason; repeats well all season.

Plant. Upright and bushy, 2½ to 4 feet, with soft, semiglossy, dark green foliage and thorny canes. Usually immune to fungus diseases. Tender.

Landscape and other uses. In beds, borders and in combination with other plants, and as cut flowers and for boutonnieres.

'PERLE D'OR'

'Pink Parfait'
Introduced 1960

Class. Grandiflora

Flowers. Double, 3½ to 4 inches, in blended tones of pink and cream, lighter toward the center. Spiraled buds open to high-centered blos-

'PINK PARFAIT'

'PINK PEACE'

'POKER CHIP'

'POPCORN'

'PRINCESSE DE MONACO'

soms that become cupped. Flowers are borne singly and in clusters. Slightly musky fragrance.

Bloom. Midseason; repeats well all season.

Plant. Upright and bushy, 3½ to 4½ feet, with semiglossy green foliage. Semihardy.

Landscape and other uses. In beds and borders, and as cut flowers.

'Pink Peace'
Introduced 1959

Class. Hybrid Tea

Flowers. Very double, 5 to 6 inches, dusky rose pink that lasts well. Spiraled buds open to cupped blossoms. Flowers are borne singly or in clusters. Strong fragrance.

Bloom. Midseason; repeats all season.

Plant. Upright, bushy and vigorous, 4½ to 5½ feet, with glossy green foliage. Semihardy.

Landscape and other uses. In beds and borders, and as cut flowers.

'Poker Chip'
Introduced 1979

Class. Miniature

Flowers. Double, 1½ inches; petals are brilliant scarlet on the upper surfaces, gold at the bases and on the undersides. Long, pointed buds open to high-centered blossoms; petals fold back to form points and show gold stamens. Flowers are borne singly or in clusters. Sweet fragrance.

Bloom. Midseason; repeats well all season.

Plant. Well-branched and vigorous, 15 to 18 inches, with glossy, dark green foliage. Semihardy.

Landscape and other uses. In beds, borders, edgings and containers, and as cut flowers and exhibition flowers.

'Popcorn'
Introduced 1973

Class. Miniature

Flowers. Semidouble, ¾ inch, white. Buds open to cupped blossoms that show prominent yellow stamens. Flowers are borne in clusters. Honey fragrance.

Bloom. Abundant in midseason; repeats well all season.

Plant. Upright and vigorous, 12 to 14 inches, with small, glossy, green foliage. Semihardy.

Landscape and other uses. In beds, borders, edgings and containers.

'Princesse de Monaco'
Introduced 1981

Class. Hybrid Tea

Flowers. Double, 4½ to 5½ inches, blended cream and pink. Round, spiraled buds open slowly to high-centered blossoms. Flowers are borne singly on short stems. Light fragrance.

Bloom. Midseason; repeats sparsely.

Plant. Upright, well-branched and vigorous, 4 to 4½ feet, with large, semiglossy, dark green foliage. Semihardy.

Landscape and other uses. In beds and borders, and as cut flowers.

'Pristine'
Introduced 1978

Class. Hybrid Tea

Flowers. Double, 4½ to 6 inches, pink shading from pale at the centers to deep at the petal edges. Long, spiraled buds open to high-centered blossoms that are short-lived. Flowers are generally borne singly. Slight fragrance.

Bloom. Midseason; repeats sparsely.

Plant. Upright and spreading, 4 to 5 feet tall, with glossy, dark reddish green foliage. Tender.

Landscape and other uses. In beds and borders, and as cut flowers and exhibition flowers.

'Queen Elizabeth'
Introduced 1954

Class. Grandiflora

Flowers. Double, 3½ to 4 inches, blended shades of soft pink. Pointed buds open to cupped blossoms. Flowers are borne singly or in clusters. Slight tea fragrance.

Bloom. Abundant in midseason; repeats well all season.

Plant. Upright and vigorous, 5 to 7 feet, with glossy, dark green foliage. Somewhat disease-resistant, and easy to grow. Semihardy.

Landscape and other uses. In beds, borders and in combination with other plants, and as cut flowers and exhibition flowers.

'Rainbow's End'
Introduced 1984

Class. Miniature

Flowers. Double, 1½ inches, yellow blending to deep pink or red where full sunlight strikes the petal edges; flowers remain pure yellow if grown in shade or indoors. Pointed buds open slowly to high-centered blossoms. Flowers are borne singly and in clusters. No fragrance.

'PRISTINE'

'QUEEN ELIZABETH'

'RAINBOW'S END'

'REDGOLD'

'RED PINOCCHIO'

'REINE DES VIOLETTES'

Bloom. Midseason; repeats all season.

Plant. Upright and bushy, 14 to 18 inches, with glossy, dark green foliage. Semihardy.

Landscape and other uses. In beds, borders, edgings and containers, and as cut flowers and exhibition flowers. Grows well indoors.

'Redgold'
Introduced 1971

Class. Floribunda

Flowers. Double, 2 to 3 inches, deep yellow, shading to deep pink or red at the petal edges on exposure to strong sunlight. Oval buds open to long-lasting, high-centered blossoms. Flowers are borne singly or in clusters. Slight fragrance.

Bloom. Midseason; repeats all season.

Plant. Upright and bushy, 3 to 3½ feet, with semiglossy, light green foliage. Semihardy.

Landscape and other uses. In beds and borders, and as cut flowers and exhibition flowers. Makes a good tree rose.

'Red Pinocchio'
Introduced 1947

Class. Floribunda

Flowers. Double, 2 to 3 inches, dark red with velvety texture. Oval buds open to cupped blossoms. Flowers are borne in large clusters. Moderate fragrance.

Bloom. Midseason; repeats all season.

Plant. Upright and spreading, 2½ to 3 feet tall, with leathery green leaves. Susceptible to mildew. Semihardy.

Landscape and other uses. In beds and borders, and as cut flowers.

'Reine des Violettes'
Introduced 1860

Class. Hybrid Perpetual

Flowers. Very double, 3 inches, lilac-red, becoming bluish violet. Buds open to cupped blossoms that expand widely to a quartered form with a button eye. The undersides of the petals are pale and silky, contrasting with darker, velvety upper surfaces. Flowers are borne singly or in small, tight clusters. Strong fragrance with a suggestion of pepper.

Bloom. Abundant in midseason; repeats sparsely at other times.

Plant. Bushy, 5 to 6 feet, with smooth, slightly gray-green foliage and nearly thornless canes. Canes are long and limber; they may be shortened to maintain a 5-foot bush, trained horizontally along a fence or pegged down to the ground to give bloom all along their length. Hardy.

Landscape and other uses. In borders and on fences.

'Rise 'n' Shine'
Introduced 1977

Class. Miniature

Flowers. Double, 1½ to 2 inches, yellow. Long, pointed buds open to high-centered blossoms. Flowers are borne singly and in clusters. Slight fragrance.

Bloom. Midseason; repeats well all season.

Plant. Upright and bushy, 14 to 16 inches, with matte green leaves. Disease-resistant. Semihardy.

Landscape and other uses. In beds, borders, edgings and containers, and as cut flowers and exhibition flowers.

'Risque'
Introduced 1985

Class. Grandiflora

Flowers. Double, 3½ inches, red and yellow. The upper petal surfaces are orange-red, the undersides light yellow. Spiraled buds open to high-centered blossoms that quickly become loose in form. Flowers are borne singly and in small clusters. No fragrance.

Bloom. Midseason; repeats all season.

Plant. Upright and slightly spreading, 3 feet tall, with semiglossy, dark green foliage. Semihardy.

Landscape and other uses. In beds and borders, and as cut flowers.

Rosa banksiae lutea, sometimes designated 'Yellow Banksian Rose'
Introduced 1824

Class. Species

Flowers. Double, 1 inch, shades of yellow, with ragged petal edges. Flowers are borne in pendent large clusters. Slight violet fragrance.

Bloom. Abundant in late spring, very early for a rose; does not repeat.

Plant. Upright, climbing and vigorous, 15 to 50 feet, with small, smooth, light green leaves and long, flexible canes. Unlike most climbing roses, which bloom on laterals, 'Yellow Banksian Rose' blooms on shoots arising from the laterals; therefore the plant is difficult to prune without sacrificing bloom. The safest course is to prune out only unproductive wood. Extremely tender; must have winter protection where temperatures fall below 15° F.

'RISE 'N' SHINE'

'RISQUE'

ROSA BANKSIAE LUTEA

139

ROSA MULTIFLORA

'ROSA MUNDI'

Landscape and other uses. On walls, fences and tree trunks.

—

Rosa damascena versicolor see 'York and Lancaster'

Rosa gallica officianalis see 'Apothecary's Rose'

—

Rosa multiflora
Introduced circa 1800

Class. Species

Flowers. Single, having five petals, ½ to ¾ inch, white with bright yellow stamens that darken and curl. Flowers are borne in large clusters. Strong, spicy, honey fragrance.

Bloom. Early midseason; does not repeat.

Plant. Arching, mounding or climbing, 6 to 15 feet, with semiglossy, light to medium green, serrated leaves and usually thorny canes. Small, round, red hips persist into winter. Birds spread the seeds freely; *Rosa multiflora* propagates itself readily and is the most common wild rose. It has been declared a noxious weed in some states. It is, however, an important ancestor of Polyanthas, Floribundas and Ramblers, and is widely used as an understock. Disease-resistant. Hardy.

Landscape and other uses. As an understock.

—

'Rosa Mundi', sometimes designated *Rosa gallica versicolor*
Introduced before 1581

Class. Gallica

Flowers. Semidouble, 3 to 3½ inches, deep pink streaks on pale pink or soft white. Buds open to wide, flat cups that effectively show off the streaking. Flowers are borne singly or in clusters of three or four on erect stems. Legend has it that 'Rosa Mundi' was named for Rosamund, the mistress of Henry II of England. It is a sport of the 'Apothecary's Rose', to which a branch will occasionally revert. Strong fragrance.

Bloom. Abundant in midseason; does not repeat.

Plant. Upright and bushy, 3 to 4 feet, with matte green leaves and almost thornless canes. Round red hips appear in late summer. Watch for and remove canes that sport back to the 'Apothecary's Rose'. Extremely hardy.

Landscape and other uses. In beds, hedges and in combination with other plants.

Rosa rugosa alba
Introduced 1870

Class. Species

Flowers. Single, having five petals, 2½ to 4 inches. Long, pointed buds are tinted blush and open quickly to pure white blossoms with creamy stamens. Flowers are generally borne in clusters. Strong clovelike fragrance.

Bloom. Early; repeats well all season.

Plant. Spreading and vigorous, 4 to 6 feet tall, with bright green, crinkled foliage. Canes are gray and extremely prickly. Large, orange-red hips form in late summer without preventing new flowers' growth; often fruit and flowers are borne side by side. *Rosa rugosa alba* grows wild in New England. It flourishes in sandy soil and salt spray and is a good rose for a seashore garden. The foliage is immune to the common rose fungus diseases and resists most insect damage. But it seems allergic to some fungicides; spare your Rugosas when spraying other roses. Extremely hardy.

Landscape and other uses. In borders, hedges and in combination with other plants, and as a specimen. The crinkled, disease-free foliage is an asset in the garden.

'Rose du Roi'
Introduced 1815

Class. Portland

Flowers. Double, 2½ to 3 inches, cherry red with darker shadings on the outer petals. Inner petals fold over into a button eye. Flowers are borne in tight clusters of three or four. Rich, strong fragrance.

Bloom. Midseason; repeats all season if well maintained.

Plant. Upright and bushy, 3 to 4 feet, with smooth green leaves borne close together just under the flowers and moderately thorny canes. Tender. Encourage repeated blooming by generous fertilizing and watering. Shorten the canes by half or two-thirds their length at spring pruning.

Landscape and other uses. In beds, borders and in combination with other plants, and as cut flowers.

'Royal Gold'
Introduced 1957

Class. Large-flowered climber

Flowers. Double, 4 inches, rich golden yellow. Oval, spiraled buds open to loose, cupped blossoms. Flowers are borne singly and in clusters. Slightly fruity fragrance.

Bloom. Light in midseason; repeats sparsely.

ROSA RUGOSA ALBA

'ROSE DU ROI'

'ROYAL GOLD'

'ROYAL HIGHNESS'

'ROYAL SUNSET'

'SEA FOAM'

Plant. Upright and vigorous, 5 to 8 feet, with glossy, dark green foliage. Tender.

Landscape and other uses. On pillars, trellises, fences and walls, and as cut flowers and exhibition flowers. Can be grown as a loose shrub without support.

'Royal Highness'
Introduced 1962

Class. Hybrid Tea

Flowers. Double, 5 to 5½ inches, light pink. Spiraled buds open slowly to high-centered blossoms. Flowers are borne singly on long stems. Strong tea fragrance.

Bloom. Midseason; repeats all season.

Plant. Upright and bushy, 4 to 5 feet, with glossy, dark green foliage. Very susceptible to rust. Tender.

Landscape and other uses. In beds and borders, and as cut flowers and exhibition flowers.

'Royal Sunset'
Introduced 1960

Class. Large-flowered climber

Flowers. Double, 4½ to 5 inches, apricot that fades in hot weather. Oval, spiraled buds open to cupped blossoms. Flowers are borne singly and in small clusters. Fruity fragrance.

Bloom. Midseason; repeats all season.

Plant. Upright, 6 to 10 feet, with glossy, deep green foliage. Tender.

Landscape and other uses. On pillars, trellises, fences and walls, and as cut flowers.

'Schneewittchen' see 'Iceberg'

'Sea Foam'
Introduced 1964

Class. Shrub

Flowers. Double, 2 to 3 inches, white shading to pink at the centers. Small round buds open to flat, cupped blossoms with short petals. Flowers are borne in clusters. Slight fragrance.

Bloom. Late midseason; repeats well all season.

Plant. Vigorous and trailing, 2½ feet in height, 8 to 12 feet in spread, with small, glossy, green foliage. Can be restricted by pruning to a 4-foot mounded shrub. Immune to fungus diseases and easy to grow. Hardy.

Landscape and other uses. In beds, borders, hedges and in combination with other plants, on pillars, as a specimen and as cut flowers. 'Sea Foam' is unusual among roses in that it can be used as a ground cover.

'Sea Pearl'
Introduced 1964

Class. Floribunda

Flowers. Double, 4½ inches, shades of pink blended with yellow and peach. Buds open slowly to high-centered blossoms. Flowers are borne singly and in small clusters. Slight fragrance.

Bloom. Early midseason; repeats all season.

Plant. Upright and bushy, 3½ to 4 feet, with semiglossy, dark green foliage. Semihardy.

Landscape and other uses. In beds and borders, and as cut flowers and exhibition flowers.

'SEA PEARL'

'Seashell'
Introduced 1976

Class. Hybrid Tea

Flowers. Double, 3½ to 4½ inches, bright coral; the color varies, being orange in cool weather and fading to pink in the hot sun. Buds open to high-centered, long-lasting blossoms. Flowers are borne singly and in clusters. Spicy tea fragrance.

Bloom. Midseason; repeats all season.

Plant. Upright and compact, 4 feet, with semiglossy, dark green foliage. Semihardy.

Landscape and other uses. In beds and borders, and as cut flowers.

'SEASHELL'

'Sheer Bliss'
Introduced 1987

Class. Hybrid Tea

Flowers. Double, 4 to 5 inches, creamy white with blush pink centers. Spiraled buds open to high-centered blossoms. Flowers are borne singly on long stems. Moderately spicy fragrance.

Bloom. Midseason; repeats all season.

Plant. Upright and bushy, 3½ to 4½ feet, with matte green leaves and thorny canes. Semihardy.

Landscape and other uses. In beds and borders, and as cut flowers.

'SHEER BLISS'

'SHOWBIZ'

'SIMPLICITY'

'SNOW BRIDE'

'Showbiz'
Introduced 1981

Class. Floribunda

Flowers. Double, 2½ to 3 inches, scarlet. Short buds open quickly to loosely cupped blossoms with ruffled petals and bright yellow stamens that darken with age. Flowers are borne in clusters. Little fragrance.

Bloom. Midseason; repeats well all season.

Plant. Compact and bushy, 2½ to 3 feet, with glossy, dark green foliage. Semihardy.

Landscape and other uses. In beds, borders and low hedges, and as cut flowers.

'Simplicity'
Introduced 1979

Class. Floribunda

Flowers. Semidouble, 3 to 4 inches, medium pink. Pointed buds open to blossoms that may be flat or cupped and show dark yellow stamens that turn light brown with age. Flowers are borne in small clusters. Little fragrance.

Bloom. Abundant in midseason; repeats well all season.

Plant. Upright and bushy, 2½ to 3½ feet, with semiglossy foliage that is light to medium green. Hardy.

Landscape and other uses. In beds, borders and hedges, and as cut flowers.

'Snow Bride'
Introduced 1982

Class. Miniature

Flowers. Double, 1½ inches, white. Long, pointed buds open to high-centered flowers that show yellow stamens. Flowers are borne singly and are long-lasting. Little fragrance.

Bloom. Midseason; repeats all season.

Plant. Compact, 18 inches, with semiglossy green foliage. Semihardy.

Landscape and other uses. In beds, borders, edgings and containers, and as cut flowers and exhibition flowers.

'Sombreuil'
Introduced 1850

Class. Climbing Tea

Flowers. Very double, 3½ to 4 inches, ivory white with distinctive beige tones toward the center. Short buds open to flat, saucer-shaped blossoms that are quartered in form. Flowers are borne in clusters on nodding stems. Strong tea fragrance.

Bloom. Midseason; repeats well.

Plant. Upright and vigorous, 8 to 12 feet, with semiglossy green leaves and moderately thorny canes. Semihardy.

Landscape and other uses. On walls, fences, trellises and arbors, and as cut flowers.

'SOMBREUIL'

'Sonia', sometimes designated 'Sonia Meilland' or 'Sweet Promise'
Introduced 1974

Class. Grandiflora

Flowers. Double, 4 to 4½ inches, pink suffused with coral. Long, slender buds open to high-centered blossoms. Flowers (which may not appear for a year after planting) are borne singly or in small clusters. Mildly fruity fragrance.

Bloom. Midseason; repeats all season.

Plant. Upright, 4 feet, with glossy, deep green foliage. Semihardy.

Landscape and other uses. In beds and borders, and as cut flowers.

'SONIA'

'Sonia Meilland' see 'Sonia'

'Stanwell Perpetual'
Introduced 1838

Class. Hybrid Spinosissima

Flowers. Double, 3 to 4 inches, blush pink fading to white. Buds open to loosely formed blossoms having many folded petals that sometimes form a button eye and obscure the buff-colored stamens. Flowers are generally borne singly on short stems. Strong fragrance.

Bloom. Early; repeats well all season after it has been established for a year or two.

Plant. Arching and spreading, 3 to 6 feet tall, with small, gray-green leaves usually consisting of seven or nine leaflets. Resistant to fungus diseases. Extremely hardy.

Landscape and other uses. In beds, borders and hedges, on banks and cascading over low walls, and as a small specimen.

'STANWELL PERPETUAL'

'STARGLO'

'STARINA'

'SUMMER SUNSHINE'

'SUNFIRE'

'Starglo'
Introduced 1973

Class. Miniature

Flowers. Double, 1¾ inches, white. Long, pointed buds open slowly to high-centered, star-shaped blossoms. Flowers are borne singly and in clusters. Slight fragrance.

Bloom. Midseason; repeats all season.

Plant. Compact, 12 to 16 inches, with semi-glossy green foliage. Semihardy.

Landscape and other uses. In beds, borders, edgings and containers, and as cut flowers and exhibition flowers.

—

'Starina'
Introduced 1965

Class. Miniature

Flowers. Double, 1½ inches, intense orange-red. Oval buds open to high-centered blossoms that become cupped and show yellow stamens. Flowers are borne in clusters. Little fragrance.

Bloom. Midseason; repeats well all season.

Plant. Upright and bushy, 15 to 18 inches, with glossy, dark green foliage. Semihardy.

Landscape and other uses. In beds, borders, edgings and containers, and as cut flowers and exhibition flowers.

—

'Summer Sunshine'
Introduced 1962

Class. Hybrid Tea

Flowers. Double, 3½ to 5 inches, deep yellow that fades quickly. Urn-shaped buds open to blossoms that may be high-centered or cupped. Flowers are borne singly. Slight fragrance.

Bloom. Midseason; repeats all season, but may not bloom well during summer heat.

Plant. Upright, 3½ to 4½ feet, with semi-glossy, gray-green foliage. Tender.

Landscape and other uses. In beds and borders, and as cut flowers.

—

'Sunfire'
Introduced 1974

Class. Floribunda

Flowers. Double, 3½ inches, bright orange-red that holds its color. Oval buds open to high-centered blossoms. Flowers are borne singly or in clusters. Slight fragrance.

Bloom. Midseason; repeats all season.

Plant. Upright and bushy, 4 feet, with leathery green foliage. Disease-resistant. Semihardy.

Landscape and other uses. In beds, borders and hedges, and as cut flowers.

'SUN FLARE'

'Sun Flare'
Introduced 1983

Class. Floribunda

Flowers. Double, 3½ inches, bright lemon yellow. Pointed buds open to flat blossoms. Flowers are generally borne in large clusters, sometimes singly. Mild licorice fragrance.

Bloom. Midseason; repeats well all season.

Plant. Slightly spreading and vigorous, 2 to 2½ feet tall, with glossy, light green foliage. Exceptionally disease-resistant; may not require any fungicide spraying. Semihardy.

Landscape and other uses. In beds, borders and in combination with other plants, and as cut flowers.

'Sunsprite'
Introduced 1977

Class. Floribunda

Flowers. Double, 3 inches, deep yellow that holds its color. Oval buds open to high-centered blossoms. Flowers are borne in clusters. Moderate to strong fragrance.

Bloom. Early midseason; repeats well throughout the season.

Plant. Compact, 3 feet, with glossy, light green leaves. Semihardy.

Landscape and other uses. In beds and borders, and as cut flowers and exhibition flowers.

'SUNSPRITE'

'Super Star' see 'Tropicana'

'Sweetheart Rose' see 'Cecile Brunner'

'Sweet Promise' see 'Sonia'

'Sweet Surrender'
Introduced 1983

Class. Hybrid Tea

Flowers. Double, 4½ to 5½ inches, silvery pink. Spiraled buds open quickly to flat blossoms with neatly overlapping, gently ruffled petals that remain folded over the centers. Flowers are usually borne singly on long stems. Strong tea scent.

'SWEET SURRENDER'

'THE FAIRY'

'TIFFANY'

'TOUCH OF CLASS'

Bloom. Midseason; repeats all season.

Plant. Upright, 4 feet, with large, matte, dark green leaves. Tender.

Landscape and other uses. In beds and borders, and as cut flowers.

'The Fairy'
Introduced 1932

Class. Polyantha

Flowers. Double, 1 to 1½ inches, light pink that turns nearly white in hot sun. Small buds open to slightly cupped blossoms that are long-lasting. No fragrance.

Bloom. Late; repeats well all season.

Plant. Spreading and vigorous, 1½ to 2½ feet tall and somewhat wider, with tiny, glossy, dark green leaves and thorny canes; usually rounded and bushy in form but sometimes trailing. Disease-resistant, but somewhat susceptible to spider mites in hot weather. Hardy.

Landscape and other uses. In beds, borders and hedges, and as cut flowers and tree roses. 'The Fairy' is among the few roses that can be used as ground cover.

'Tiffany'
Introduced 1954

Class. Hybrid Tea

Flowers. Double, 4 to 5 inches, soft rose pink with a glow of yellow at the petal bases. Long, pointed buds open to high-centered blossoms. Flowers are borne singly or in clusters. Strong old-rose fragrance.

Bloom. Midseason; repeats well all season.

Plant. Upright and bushy, 4½ feet, with glossy, dark green foliage. More disease-resistant than most hybrid teas. Performs best where summers are hot. Semihardy.

Landscape and other uses. In beds and borders, and as cut flowers.

'Toro' see 'Uncle Joe'

'Touch of Class'
Introduced 1986

Class. Hybrid Tea

Flowers. Double, 4½ to 5½ inches, pink blended with cream and coral. Spiraled buds open to high-centered blossoms. Flowers are generally borne singly on long stems. Slight fragrance.

Bloom. Midseason; repeats all season.

Plant. Upright, 4 feet, with small, semiglossy, dark green leaves. Semihardy.

Landscape and other uses. In beds and borders, and as cut flowers.

—

'Tropicana', sometimes designated
'Super Star'
Introduced 1960

Class. Hybrid Tea

Flowers. Double, 4 to 5 inches, brilliant orange-red that holds its color and shows up brightly from a great distance. Pointed buds open to blossoms that are high-centered at first and later become cup-shaped. Flowers are borne singly. Strong fruity fragrance.

Bloom. Midseason; repeats well all season.

Plant. Upright, 4 to 5 feet, with glossy, dark green foliage. Susceptible to mildew. Semihardy.

Landscape and other uses. In beds and borders, and as cut flowers.

—

'Trumpeter'
Introduced 1977

Class. Floribunda

Flowers. Double, 3½ inches, vivid scarlet that holds its color well even in hot sun. Oval buds open to high-centered blooms. Flowers are borne singly and in clusters. Slight fragrance.

Bloom. Abundant in midseason; repeats well all season.

Plant. Upright and bushy, 3 to 4½ feet, with glossy, dark green foliage. Semihardy.

Landscape and other uses. In beds, borders and hedges, and as cut flowers.

—

'Uncle Joe', sometimes designated 'Toro'
Introduced 1971

Class. Hybrid Tea

Flowers. Very double, 6 inches, medium to dark red. Buds open slowly to high-centered blossoms. Flowers are borne singly on long stems. Cool, damp weather sometimes stunts flower production. Strong fragrance.

Bloom. Midseason; repeats all season.

Plant. Upright, 5 feet, with glossy, dark green foliage. Semihardy.

Landscape and other uses. In beds and borders, and as cut flowers.

'TROPICANA'

'TRUMPETER'

'UNCLE JOE'

'VARIEGATA DI BOLOGNA'

'WHITE DAWN'

'WHITE LIGHTNIN'

'Variegata di Bologna'
Introduced 1909

Class. Bourbon

Flowers. Very double, 3 to 4 inches, striped crimson or wine on white. Short buds open to cupped, globular blossoms. Flowers are borne in clusters. Strong fragrance.

Bloom. Abundant in midseason; repeats sparsely or not at all.

Plant. Upright, 5 to 8 feet, with semiglossy green foliage and few thorns. Canes are long and limber; they may be trained to climb, pegged down to the ground, or pruned severely to form a compact bush of 4 or 5 feet. Susceptible to black spot. Hardy.

Landscape and other uses. In borders, on fences and trellises, as a specimen and as cut flowers.

—

'White Dawn'
Introduced 1949

Class. Large-flowered climber

Flowers. Double, 2 to 3 inches, white. Short buds open to flat blossoms. Flowers are borne in clusters. Moderate fragrance.

Bloom. Midseason; repeats all season.

Plant. Vigorous, 8 to 12 feet, with glossy, dark green leaves. Hardy.

Landscape and other uses. On pillars, trellises, fences and walls.

—

'White Lightnin'
Introduced 1980

Class. Grandiflora

Flowers. Double, 3 to 4 inches, white. Pointed buds open to cupped blossoms. Flowers are borne singly and in small clusters. Strong citrus fragrance.

Bloom. Midseason; repeats well all season.

Plant. Upright and bushy, 4 to 5 feet, with glossy, dark green foliage. Semihardy.

Landscape and other uses. In beds and borders, and as cut flowers.

—

'Yellow Banksian Rose'
see *Rosa banksiae lutea*

'Yellow Doll'

Introduced 1962

Class. Miniature

Flowers. Double, 1½ inches, yellow that fades to cream. Pointed buds open to high-centered blossoms. Flowers are borne singly or in clusters. Slight fragrance.

Bloom. Midseason; repeats all season.

Plant. Compact and vigorous, 8 to 10 inches, with glossy, dark green foliage. Semihardy.

Landscape and other uses. In beds, borders, edgings and containers.

'YELLOW DOLL'

—

'York and Lancaster', sometimes designated *Rosa damascena versicolor*

Introduced before 1551

Class. Damask

Flowers. Double, 2 to 3 inches, all white, all pink, or white and pink combined. Moderate fragrance. The flower is named for the adversaries in the Wars of the Roses in 15th-century England; the white rose was the symbol of the royal house of York and the red rose the symbol of the royal house of Lancaster. Buds open to loosely cupped blossoms. Flowers are borne in clusters.

Bloom. Midseason; does not repeat.

Plant. Upright and bushy, 3 to 5 feet, with slightly gray-green leaves and thorny canes. Difficult to grow; needs cool conditions and good soil. Extremely hardy.

Landscape and other uses. In borders and in combination with other plants.

'YORK AND LANCASTER'

PICTURE CREDITS

The sources for the illustrations in this book are listed below. Cover photograph of 'Gold Medal' rose by Thomas Eltzroth. Watercolor paintings by Nicholas Fasciano and Yin Yi except pages 22, 23, 24, 25, 26, 27, 28, 29: Lorraine Moseley Epstein and Yin Yi. 94, 95, 96, 97: Lorraine Moseley Epstein. Maps on pages 88, 89, 91, 93: digitized by Richard Furno, inked by John Drummond.

Frontispiece paintings listed by page number: 6: *Persian Rose Bush,* c. 1975 by Fairfield Porter. Courtesy Mr. and Mrs. Austin List, photo courtesy Hirschl & Adler Modern, New York. 30: *Roses, Garden at Petit-Gennevilliers,* c. 1886 by Gustave Caillebotte. Private collection, photo courtesy BL-Giraudon, Paris. 50: *Pink Roses with Wasps,* detail, Chinese scroll, Ch'ing dynasty, 1644-1911, artist unknown. Courtesy Metropolitan Museum of Art, Fletcher Fund (47.18.5). 72: *Bowl of Wild Roses,* c. 1880 by John LaFarge. Courtesy Museum of Fine Arts, Boston, bequest of Elizabeth Howard Bartol.

Photographs in Chapters 1 through 4 from the following sources, listed by page number: 8: Horticultural Photography, Corvallis, OR. 10: Thomas Eltzroth. 14: Pamela Harper. 16: Horticultural Photography, Corvallis, OR. 18: Pamela Zilly. 20: Pamela Harper. 22: Maggie Oster. 32: Horticultural Photography, Corvallis, OR. 34: Thomas Eltzroth. 36: Joy Spurr. 38: Renée Comet. 40: Saxon Holt. 44: Pamela Harper. 46: Robert Lyons. 48: Mark Gibson. 52: Pamela Zilly. 56: Renée Comet. 58: Robert Lowe. 60: Horticultural Photography, Corvallis, OR. 64: Pamela Zilly. 68: Mike Lowe. 70: Jack Potter. 74: Fil Hunter. 76: Pamela Zilly. 78: Fil Hunter. 80: Robert Lowe. 84: Pamela Zilly.

Photographs in the Dictionary of Roses from the following sources, listed by page and numbered from top to bottom. Page 102, 1: Jack Potter; 2: Robert Lowe; 3: Pamela Harper. 103, 1, 2: Thomas Eltzroth; 3: Jack Potter. 104, 1: Jack Potter; 2, 3: Thomas Eltzroth. 105, 1, 2: Thomas Eltzroth; 3: Sweetbriar Press, Palo Alto, California. 106, 1: Joy Spurr; 2: Joanne Pavia. 107, 1, 2: Jack Potter; 3: Thomas Eltzroth. 108, 1: Al Thompson; 2: Jack Potter; 3: Alice Garik; 4: Connie Toops. 109, 1: Maggie Oster; 2: Roses of Yesterday and Today, Watsonville, California; 3: Thomas Eltzroth. 110, 1: Bob Grant; 2: Thomas Eltzroth; 3: Horticultural Photography, Corvallis, OR. 111, 1: Thomas Eltzroth; 2: Jack Potter; 3: Alice Garik. 112, 1: Robert Lowe; 2: Thomas Eltzroth; 3: Saxon Holt. 113, 1: Saxon Holt; 2: Horticultural Photography, Corvallis, OR.; 3: Joy Spurr; 4: Jack Potter. 114, 1: Derek Fell; 2: Thomas Eltzroth; 3: Pamela Harper. 115, 1, 2, 3: Jack Potter; 4: Thomas Eltzroth. 116, 1: Thomas Eltzroth; 2: Jack Potter; 3: Thomas Eltzroth. 117, 1: Joanne Pavia; 2: Thomas Eltzroth; 3: Robert Lowe. 118, 1, 2: Thomas Eltzroth; 3: Horticultural Photography, Corvallis, OR.; 4: Jack Potter. 119, 1: Jack Potter; 2: Pamela Harper; 3: Joanne Pavia. 120, 1, 2, 3: Thomas Eltzroth. 121, 1, 2: Pamela Harper; 3: Bear Creek Gardens, Somis, California. 122, 1: Jack Potter; 2: Thomas Eltzroth; 3: Jack Potter. 123, 1: Jack Potter; 2: Pamela Harper; 3: Thomas Eltzroth; 4: Robert Lowe. 124, 1: Thomas Eltzroth; 2: Bob Grant; 3: Thomas Eltzroth. 125, 1, 2, 3: Jack Potter. 126, 1: Alice Garik; 2: Sweetbriar Press, Palo Alto, California; 3: Robert Lowe; 4: Jack Potter. 127, 1: Alice Garik; 2: Maggie Oster; 3: Roses of Yesterday and Today, Watsonville, California. 128, 1: Robert Lowe; 2: Albert H. Ford; 3: Saxon Holt. 129, 1: Jack Potter; 2: Thomas Eltzroth; 3: Saxon Holt. 130, 1: Jack Potter; 2, 3: Thomas Eltzroth. 131, 1, 2: Robert Lowe; 3: Jack Potter. 132, 1: Joy Spurr; 2, 3: Pamela Harper. 133, 1: Robert Lowe; 2: Jack Potter; 3: Thomas Eltzroth; 4: Maggie Oster. 134, 1: Saxon Holt; 2: Robert Lowe; 3: Thomas Eltzroth. 135, 1: Joanne Pavia; 2: Thomas Eltzroth; 3: Jack Potter; 4: Saxon Holt. 136, 1: Thomas Eltzroth; 2: Robert Lowe; 3: Pamela Harper; 4: Robert Alde. 137, 1: Horticultural Photography, Corvallis, OR.; 2: Thomas Eltzroth; 3: Alice Garik. 138, 1: Thomas Eltzroth; 2: Alice Garik; 3: Charles Bell. 139, 1: Joy Spurr; 2, 3: Thomas Eltzroth. 140, 1: Jack Potter; 2: Robert Alde. 141, 1: Bob Grant; 2: Stephen Scanniello/ Brooklyn Botanic Garden; 3: Alice Garik. 142, 1: Robert Lowe; 2: Jerry Pavia; 3: Robert Lowe. 143, 1: P. A. Haring; 2: Connie Toops; 3: Alice Garik. 144, 1: Gottlieb Hampfler; 2, 3: Thomas Eltzroth. 145, 1: Jack Potter; 2: Robert Lowe; 3: Jack Potter. 146, 1: Maggie Oster; 2: Horticultural Photogrpahy, Corvallis, OR.; 3: Bob Grant; 4: Thomas Eltzroth. 147, 1: Jack Potter; 2: Horticultural Photography, Corvallis, OR.; 3: Jack Potter. 148, 1: Pamela Harper; 2: Jack Potter; 3: Alice Garik. 149, 1: Connie Toops; 2: Pamela Harper; 3: Ann Reilly. 150, 1: Pamela Harper; 2: Jack Potter; 3: Stephen Scanniello/Brooklyn Botanic Garden. 151, 1: Saxon Holt; 2: Jack Potter.

ACKNOWLEDGMENTS

The index for this book was prepared by Lee McKee.
The editors also wish to thank: Robert Alde, President, Potomac Rose Society, Rockville, Maryland; Lynn Baden, American Rose Society, Shreveport, Louisiana; Richard Barse, Rockville, Maryland; Charles Bell, Alexandria, Virginia; Joe Borras, Accokeek, Maryland; Filoli Gardens, Woodside, California; Gen Flanagan, St. Cloud, Minnesota; Betsy Frankel, Alexandria, Virginia; Bob Gold, Seattle, Washington; Leon E. Greene, Fairfax, Virginia; Ed Griffith, Mobile, Alabama; Kay Halfhill, Lompoc, California; Kenneth E. Hancock, Annandale, Virginia; Michael Harris, Division of Medical Science, Smithsonian Institution, Washington, D.C.; Heritage House of Old Town, Alexandria, Virginia; Gregory Higby, Director of Pharmacy History, University of Wisconsin, Madison, Wisconsin; Floyd Johnson, Wauwatosa, Wisconsin; Lisa Johnson, Blossoms & Bows Company, Alexandria, Virginia; Kay and Bud Jones, Santa Barbara, California; Robert Lowe, President, Chesapeake Rose Society, Baltimore, Maryland; Linda Morris, Baltimore, Maryland; Sandie Morris, St. Joseph, Missouri; Jerry Mountain, Mankato, Minnesota; Jayne E. Rohrich, Alexandria, Virginia; Lucille Shifrin, Gaithersburg, Maryland; Candace Scott, College Park, Maryland.

FURTHER READING

American Rose Society, *Modern Roses 9.* Shreveport, Louisiana: American Rose Society, 1986.

Bailey, Liberty Hyde, and Ethel Zoe Bailey, *Hortus Third: A Concise Dictionary of Plants Cultivated in the United States and Canada.* New York: Macmillan, 1976.

Beales, Peter, *Classic Roses.* New York: Holt, Rinehart and Winston, 1985.

Bunyard, Edward A., *Old Garden Roses.* Crugers, New York: Earl M. Coleman Enterprises, 1978 (reprint of 1936 edition).

Burst, Robert, *The Rose Manual.* Crugers, New York: Earl M. Coleman Enterprises, 1978 (reprint of 1844 edition).

Dobson, Beverly, *Combined Rose List 1988.* Irvington, New York: Beverly R. Dobson (215 Harriman Road, Irvington, New York 10533).

Fitch, Charles M., *The Complete Book of Miniature Roses.* New York: Hawthorn Books, 1977.

Gault, S. Millar, and Patrick M. Synge, *The Dictionary of Roses in Colour.* London: Michael Joseph, 1985.

Gore, Catherine F., *The Book of Roses or The Rose Fancier's Manual.* Crugers, New York: Earl M. Coleman Enterprises, 1978 (reprint of 1838 edition).

Hamilton, Geoff, *The Organic Garden Book.* New York: Crown Publishers, 1987.

Harkness, J. C., *Favorite Roses of the World.* New York: McGraw-Hill, 1979.

Hillier, Malcolm, and Colin Hilton, *The Complete Book of Dried Flowers.* London: Dorling Kindersley, 1986.

Horst, A. Kenneth, *Compendium of Rose Diseases.* St. Paul, Minnesota: American Phytopathological Society, 1983.

Keays, Ethelyn Emery, *Old Roses.* Crugers, New York: Earl M. Coleman Enterprises, 1978 (reprint of 1935 edition).

McCann, Sean, *Miniature Roses for Home and Garden.* New York: Arco Publishing, 1985.

McGredy, Sam, and Sean Jennett, *A Family of Roses.* New York: Dodd, Mead, 1971.

McNair, James K., *All about Roses.* San Francisco: Ortho Books/Chevron Chemical Company, 1976.

Malins, Peter, and M. M. Graf, *Peter Malins' Rose Book.* New York: Dodd, Mead, 1979.

Nisbet, Fred J., *Growing Better Roses.* New York: Alfred A. Knopf, 1973.

Organic Gardening magazine, *The Encyclopedia of Organic Gardening.* Emmaus, Pennsylvania: Rodale Press, 1978.

Paul, William, *The Rose Garden.* Crugers, New York: Earl M. Coleman Enterprises, 1978 (reprint of 1848 edition).

Phillips, Roger, and Martyn Rix, *Roses.* New York: Random House, 1988.

Ray, Richard, and Michael MacCaskey, *Roses: How to Select, Grow and Enjoy.* Tucson, Arizona: HP Books, 1985.

Reddell, Rayford Clayton, *Growing Good Roses.* New York: Harper & Row, 1988.

Reilly, Ann, *Roses You Can Grow.* Des Moines, Iowa: Better Homes and Gardens, 1978.

Rockwell, F. F., and Esther C. Grayson, *The Rockwells' Complete Book of Roses.* New York: Doubleday, 1966.

Shepherd, Roy E., *History of the Rose.* Crugers, New York: Earl M. Coleman Enterprises, 1978 (reprint of 1954 edition).

Smith, Michael D., ed., *The Ortho Problem Solver.* San Francisco: Ortho Books/Chevron Chemical Company, 1984.

Steen, Nancy, *The Charm of Old Roses.* Washington, D.C.: Milldale Press, 1987.

Taylor, Norman, *Taylor's Guide to Roses.* Boston: Houghton Mifflin, 1976.

Thomas, Graham Stuart:
   Climbing Roses, Old and New. London: J. M. Dent and Sons, 1983.
   The Old Shrub Roses. London: J. M. Dent and Sons, 1980.
   Shrub Roses of Today. London: J. M. Dent and Sons, 1978.

Thomson, Richard, *Old Roses for Modern Gardens.* Princeton, New Jersey: D. Van Nostrand, 1959.

Warner, Christopher, *Climbing Roses.* London: Century Hutchinson, 1987.

Wescott, Cynthia, *The Gardener's Bug Book.* New York: Doubleday, 1973.

Wilson, Helen van Pelt, and Leonie Bell, *The Fragrant Year.* New York: William Morrow, 1967.

INDEX

REDEFINITION

Senior Editors	Anne Horan, Robert G. Mason
Design Director	Robert Barkin
Designer	Edwina Smith
Illustration	Nicholas Fasciano
Assistant Designers	Sue Pratt, Monique Strawderman
Picture Editor	Deborah Thornton
Production Editor	Anthony K. Pordes
Editorial Research	Gail Prensky (volume coordinator), Barbara B. Smith, Mary Yee, Elizabeth D. McLean
Text Editor	Sharon Cygan
Writers	Gerald Jonas, Jack Potter, Ann Reilly, David S. Thomson
Administrative Assistant	Margaret M. Higgins
Business Manager	Catherine M. Chase
PRESIDENT	Edward Brash

Time-Life Books Inc.
is a wholly owned subsidiary of

TIME INCORPORATED

FOUNDER	Henry R. Luce 1898-1967
Editor-in-Chief	Jason McManus
Chairman and Chief Executive Officer	J. Richard Munro
President and Chief Operating Officer	N. J. Nicholas Jr.
Editorial Director	Ray Cave
Executive Vice President, Books	Kelso F. Sutton
Vice President, Books	Paul V. McLaughlin

TIME-LIFE BOOKS INC.

EDITOR	George Constable
Executive Editor	Ellen Phillips
Director of Design	Louis Klein
Director of Editorial Resources	Phyllis K. Wise
Editorial Board	Russell B. Adams Jr., Dale M. Brown, Roberta Conlan, Thomas H. Flaherty, Lee Hassig, Donia Ann Steele, Rosalind Stubenberg
Director of Photography and Research	John Conrad Weiser
Assistant Director of Editorial Resources	Elise Ritter Gibson
PRESIDENT	Christopher T. Linen
Chief Operating Officer	John M. Fahey Jr.
Senior Vice Presidents	Robert M. DeSena, James L. Mercer, Paul R. Stewart
Vice Presidents	Stephen L. Bair, Ralph J. Cuomo, Neal Goff, Stephen L. Goldstein, Juanita T. James, Hallett Johnson III, Carol Kaplan, Susan J. Maruyama, Robert H. Smith, Joseph J. Ward
Director of Production Services	Robert J. Passantino
Supervisor of Quality Control	James King

Editorial Operations

Copy Chief	Diane Ullius
Production	Celia Beattie
Library	Louise D. Forstall
Correspondents	Elisabeth Kraemer-Singh (Bonn), Maria Vincenza Aloisi (Paris), Ann Natanson (Rome)

THE CONSULTANTS

C. Colston Burrell is the series consultant for The Time-Life Gardener's Guide. He is Curator of Plant Collections at the Minnesota Landscape Arboretum, part of the University of Minnesota.

Albert L. Thompson, consultant for *Roses,* has raised and studied roses in locations from the Midwest to the Pacific Coast for more than 30 years. He writes a weekly gardening column for a newspaper in Lompoc, California, and is a consultant to several rose societies.

Library of Congress Cataloging-in-Publication Data
Roses.
    p. cm.—(The Time-Life gardener's guide)
    Bibliograpy: p.
    Includes index.
    1. Rose culture.   2. Roses.
I. Time-Life Books. II. Series.
SB411.R6599 1989 635.9'33372—dc19 88-29484 CIP
ISBN 0-8094-6628-7.
ISBN 0-8094-6629-5 (lib. bdg.)

Time-Life Books Inc. offers a wide range of fine recordings, including a *Rock 'n' Roll Era* series. For subscription information, call 1-800-621-7026, or write Time-Life Music, P.O. Box C-32068, Richmond, Virginia 23261-2068.